INSIDE THE WORLD OF THE KRAYS
MURDER
WITHOUT CONVICTION

Published by John Blake Publishing Ltd,
3 Bramber Court, 2 Bramber Road,
London W14 9PB, England

www.johnblakepublishing.co.uk

First published in hardback by Sidgwick & Jackson, 1986
Published in paperback by Sphere Books Ltd, 1988
This edition by John Blake Publishing, 2010

ISBN: 978 1 84454 983 2

British Library Cataloguing-in-Publication Data:
A catalogue record for this book is available from the British Library.

Design by www.envydesign.co.uk

Printed in Great Britain by CPI Bookmarque, Croydon CRO 4TD

1 3 5 7 9 10 8 6 4 2

Papers used by John Blake Publishing are natural, recyclable products made
from wood grown in sustainable forests. The manufacturing processes
conform to the environmental regulations of the country of origin.

INSIDE THE WORLD OF THE KRAYS
MURDER
WITHOUT CONVICTION

JOHN DICKSON

JOHN BLAKE

AUTHOR'S NOTE

I would like to thank Tony Peake for having confidence in this book from the beginning.

CONTENTS

*To my wife, who showed such understanding when
I told her I would like to write my account of the
events that took place between 1964 and 1968*

CHAPTER 1

TO LONDON

This is a true story about what happened to two young men, who in 1964 left their homes in Edinburgh and travelled down to London. They hoped to start a new life in the big city but ended up getting involved with the most violent gang in the East End. They were a bit like flies which got caught in a spider's web: once in it was difficult to get out. I was one of those young men who got caught inextricably.

But first we must go back to the very beginning. I was born in the docklands of Leith, Edinburgh – one of a family of eight. I left school at fourteen and started to work for a local engineering firm. On reaching my eighteenth birthday, however, I began to seek adventure and volunteered to join the Royal Marines. I trained for two years at the Commando

School in Lympstone, Devon, where we were prepared for active service. Amongst other things, this entailed learning how to use small arms and doing a course in judo. Then I joined up with 45 Commando and was shipped out to Malaya to fight the terrorists. Following that, I volunteered to join HMS *Newcastle* to fight in the Korean War. I travelled the world with the *Newcastle* and received three campaign medals: one for Malaya, one for Korea and a United Nations medal.

I came out of the Marines in 1955, and went back home to my family in Scotland. I tried to settle down to civilian life and didn't have much trouble finding a job – first as a 'rigger' for the Scottish Gas Board (setting up equipment for the engineers), then working with heavy machinery on a conveyor-type system for a local engineering company – but the routine was monotonous. I even tried going out on the trawlers, but it was no good; I just felt that after twelve years of service, and travelling halfway round the world, Scotland was small and uninteresting.

Years passed. I had spent a few of my leaves from the Marines in London and by 1964 I had begun to toy with the idea of going there to try my luck. One evening while I was chewing these thoughts over in my mind, I met a couple of my old pre-service-days friends and we all went out for a drink. They had somebody with them whom I had never met before and they introduced him to me as Ian. He was roughly five-feet ten-inches tall (taller than me), slim built with dark brown curly hair. One side of his face was scarred due to petrol blowing up in his face when he was in the army but this didn't stop women finding him attractive. He was a quiet-spoken man, but he looked tough and we got on well together. He could obviously handle himself. He told me he worked for Salvesons Shipping Company in Leith. He was a deckhand on a factory ship which went out to sea and waited for the smaller boats to bring in their catch of whales, which they gutted before fetching them back to the docks.

Ian and I had a lot in common: we were both bachelors and we had both been out with the fishing boats. We became pals and often went out drinking together. After some months had passed I told him that I had been thinking of leaving Scotland and going down to London. He told me that he had been thinking the very same thing. He, too, was bored with the slow pace and wondered whether maybe London would provide us with what we restlessly felt was lacking in our lives.

So we decided to leave Scotland. We made

arrangements to quit our jobs and told our respective families of our decision to start a new life in London. I was thirty-four years old. We said our goodbyes, promised to keep in touch and got the train to King's Cross Station.

We arrived full of high hopes and got off to a good start: on the first morning we found accommodation in a boarding house in York Road, in the heart of King's Cross. Dominated by two railway stations (King's Cross and St Pancras) the area was drab and rather depressing and populated in those days by the Irish and Scots who came to London in order to find work and better themselves. After Edinburgh, with its clean and elegant streets and gardens, and its historic castle teeming with tourists in the summer, King's Cross came as quite a blow.

Two weeks later we decided to move on to a slightly smarter part of town – Stoke Newington in North London. Before the war it had obviously been quite a smart area, consisting of large houses and wide tree-lined streets. By the '60s, however, it was well on the way to decline and was rapidly becoming cosmopolitan and full of bedsits. A sign saying 'Rooms Vacant' in a shop window led to us moving into two furnished rooms over a window-cleaning company. In exchange for the room we worked as window cleaners. After a couple of months my landlord – who knew I could drive – offered me a job as a driving instructor.

Once we had started earning money we began frequenting the local card clubs. I was not only a good card player but also a lucky one, and with Ian backing my play we won enough money to supplement what we earned.

After we had been in London about four months one of our colleagues at work told us about a card club he knew in the East End. He often played there and we thought it worth a game or two. It was situated above some shops in Brick Lane. We could see this was a very old part of London, and it was also very shabby: the streets were narrow and full of cottage-style houses, some of which were hopelessly overcrowded and little more than slums. The people who lived there included a lot of immigrants (in the 1900s it had been a haven for Poles and Russians), and over the years it had become the heart of the dress- and coat-making industry. As we walked through the back streets I couldn't help thinking of Jack the Ripper who had stalked these same roads in the 1880s.

To reach the club we had to walk up a very dark and narrow staircase. It was one of several illegal gaming clubs in the East End at the time: it was privately owned and unlicensed and you had to pay to enter. A man stood at the door to warn players of a possible raid by police. Inside you were served with tea and snacks and the most popular games were rummy and kalooki (a form of rummy played with thirteen cards). As we entered, the men (many of whom seemed to be businessmen) all stopped playing and looked over to us. I saw them grab their money off the table and shove it in their pockets. Later on we were told that they thought we were 'the law' doing the rounds – apparently it was illegal to have money on the tables.

The manager came over to us. He looked extremely nervous but was very friendly. 'Can I help you?' he asked. 'I am sorry, but this is a private club and only members are permitted to play. Someone must sign you in, they are the rules.'

We didn't think it likely that anybody would sign us in, so we said 'OK', and made for the door. At that point, a short man in his fifties came over to us, smoking a cigar almost as big as himself. 'I am his partner,' he said, pointing to the manager. 'Anything I can do for you?'

I told him that we had come down from Scotland a few months ago. 'And we don't know anybody in London.'

He told us the rules of the club and said: 'Now that you are here, would you both like some tea?' Before we had a chance to answer he shouted over to an old, Polish gent. 'Alphonse! Two teas over here.'

After talking to us for about fifteen minutes about the East End, he called the manager over and whispered something to him. Then he said: 'I will sign you both in. I am Billy Kray, what's your names?' He indicated a members' book, and we introduced ourselves and got signed in.

We had never heard the name Kray before. But after a few meetings with our new friend we heard from the other card players about the Kray twins. Apparently, they had an interest in the backstreet gaming clubs and Billy looked after the firm's interest in the club in Brick Lane. Being a keen gambler, he tended, however, to gamble with the money from the club that should have gone to the twins. Billy was their uncle.

We went out most evenings with Billy after that, and found him to be a rather heavy drinker, but he was a very generous man and we regarded him as a good friend. He was noisy but likeable. We also went quite regularly to his club, having no other social life at that time. One evening at about eight o'clock, we met Billy as usual in the club.

'Do you fancy coming for a drink?' he asked. 'I would like you to meet my two nephews, Ronnie and Reggie.'

We looked at each other and said almost together, 'Why not?'

Had we known then what we were getting into, we might not have agreed quite so readily.

Ian couldn't drive, and I hadn't yet bought a car, so we all got into Billy's old banger and drove the couple of miles to Whitechapel, where Billy parked the car in a side street and we walked to the Grave Maurice, a pub in the High Street.

It was very dimly lit inside, and when I looked around I felt as though I had walked right onto a film set with Al Capone and his gang. There were small groups of men talking and drinking, some were standing at the bar, and some were seated at small tables. All appeared to be wearing £100 suits.

There was one man sitting at a table apart from all the others. He was dark-haired, smartly dressed in suit and tie and stockily built, and was talking very earnestly to a rather elderly looking man, whom I learned later was a lawyer from Fleet Street. Billy turned to us and, indicating the younger of the two men at the table, said: 'That dark young man is my nephew, Ronnie.'

As we looked across the bar, Ronnie peered up over his glasses. He looked serious and commanding. He glanced at us and at his uncle, then he called over to one of the men standing at the bar and told him to get Billy, Ian and myself a drink. We assumed, quite wrongly, that he had been expecting us.

Up to this point, the rest of the 'firm', as we were told to call them, had been standing and watching us in a not very welcoming way. I looked at one of them in particular, who had a scar down the right side of his face. I thought to myself, 'My God, he does look terrible.' I was to find out much later that he was paying the firm for protection for his club, and tonight was paying-in night for him.

After Ronnie offered us drinks the men relaxed. Then Reggie came over to us. We both knew who he was immediately because of his striking likeness to Ronnie, though he was slightly slimmer and better looking. He smiled and shook hands with us, and I felt that he was friendlier, more relaxed and more sociable than his brother. He was just as smartly dressed and he smoked just as heavily. Billy introduced us, calling us his friends.

At first, Reggie didn't seem too sure of us and we just exchanged small talk for a time. But after a while he seemed to loosen up and told Ian and me that he had quite a few friends from Glasgow (the penny didn't seem to drop that we were from Edinburgh). He pointed to a big, eighteen-stone man, who apparently always sat near the door of the pub. 'He's from Glasgow,' he said. 'He's a big fat slob who will not go on a diet.' Reggie said this jokingly because 'Big Pat' was a friendly guy and likeable.

Reggie then told us that he and his brother had interests in gaming clubs in both the East and West Ends of London. Pointing to his uncle he added: 'The one he is in belongs to us, he's an old drunken bastard but we look after him, right Billy?' Billy nodded, but made no reply. Reggie laughed as he told us that Billy frequently 'lost' some of the money from the club.

He then went on to explain to us that there had been quite a bit of bother in the past with a few Glasgow gangsters coming down to London, trying to muscle in on the firm's interests. 'They have never been back, they got well sorted out,' he said, leaving it to our imagination as to what 'sorted out' entailed.

I quickly said: 'The first club we have ever been in is the one where your uncle works.'

Reggie called for some more drinks, and then he said: 'See you later.' He turned away from us and started roaming around the bar, talking to various members of the firm. He had an unusual habit of putting his hands on people's shoulders while he was speaking to them. He obviously enjoyed feeling he could command and control other people.

Ian and I were left alone at the bar for a time. I looked around me and thought that it looked like some sort of secret society, with men coming into the pub and 'Big Pat' acknowledging them with a nod at the door. He certainly seemed to know them all. 'What do you think of this pub?' I asked.

'I am not sure I like the fucking atmosphere here,' he replied. 'Shall we have it away?'

Just then Ronnie called over a member of the firm and whispered something to him. The man went outside for a few minutes and when he came back into the bar he nodded to Ronnie, who then said his goodbyes to the elderly man he had been speaking to. (We learned later that it was a recognized routine for someone to go outside to check that there were no police around before an 'influential' person left the pub after a meeting with the firm.)

Ronnie got up from his table and came over to where Ian and I were still standing. He stared directly at us with penetrating eyes but he did not shake hands with us. Instead, he turned to his uncle. 'You are fucking drunk again,' he said, smiling sarcastically.

11

Before Billy could answer Ronnie went on impatiently, 'Why didn't you tell me first, that you were bringing some people here tonight?'

Billy mumbled that we were good pals of his and that he thought it would be OK. He was clearly nervous in Ronnie's company.

Apparently Ronnie objected to anybody bringing strangers into his company without asking him first. He didn't forget that Billy had disobeyed the rules, because the following evening when we went to the card club, Billy told us that he must forfeit one month's wages out of what the twins were paying him to look after their interests in the club. Ronnie's temper was, we could tell, something to be reckoned with.

CHAPTER 2

JOINING THE FIRM

In the course of the next few weeks we were invited back to the pub for drinks, but we were always accompanied by Billy. We started getting on first-name terms with some of the firm and after the pub closed we were sometimes invited to go to various nightspots in the West End. This was a new world to us – wining and dining and being paid for by the firm.

One evening Ian and I were at the club playing cards when the phone rang. The manager came over to where we were sitting and whispered to Ian: 'Ronnie Kray wants to see you both in the pub to have a few drinks and a chat. He wants you to go early, before the others come in. Don't take Billy, go on your own.'

Ian came round to my side of the table and repeated the message to me.

We played a few more games of cards, and when we got up and went to get our jackets the manager said: 'You had better get there early, because it puts Ronnie in a lousy mood if he is kept waiting.'

It was about 7.30 so we got over to the pub fast.

Ronnie was already there when we arrived, and 'Big Pat' was in his usual place by the door. As we walked into the bar Pat said: 'Ron is in the Gents; he will be with you in a minute.'

We both stood at the bar and Pat called to the barman, 'Give them a drink.'

Just then Ronnie came into the bar. 'Come over here boys,' he called, 'I want to have a chat with you.'

He sat down at the same table he had used on the night we had first seen him. This, we were told later, was the 'meeting table', and only he ever used it, the reason being that he could always see the door. He would look up every time the door opened so he always knew who was in the pub whenever he was there.

He was in a very good mood and I reckoned it was due to the fact that he had a good-looking boy of about nineteen sitting with him. It was common knowledge that he liked to have young men around him. The boy's name was David and Ronnie asked him if he would mind sitting at the bar while he had a chat with Ian and myself.

He asked exactly the same questions that his brother Reggie had asked the first time we met – about villains in Scotland and whether we knew any. (The only villains I knew about were the ones whose names appeared in the daily papers – but I didn't tell him that.) He also seemed interested to know what we did for a living.

'I work for an Irish family,' I told him. 'They have a place in Stoke Newington and I do a lot of driving for them. They are very good to us. Ian works at window cleaning and sometimes he does a bit of work on their cars for them. It suits us because they let us live there and they don't take any dig money from us.'

'That all sounds fucking boring,' Ronnie said. 'How would you both like to be with the firm?'

We stared at him in amazement. This was the last thing we had expected. After all, we had only known the brothers for a short time and up until now we had been very green about London's underworld – all it consisted of, as far as we knew, was illegal gaming clubs. We were just two young workers getting our wages every week and living well.

'What would we be doing?' asked Ian.

'Just what you are doing now,' Ronnie replied. 'Drinking, and going with me wherever I have to go. I need men who can handle themselves. We have a lot of interests in clubs all over London, and sometimes we run into a bit of bother. You both look as though you can handle a bit of aggro.'

Things were starting to look interesting, so we agreed.

Just then Reggie came into the bar with his minder, who sat down at the door next to Pat. Reggie walked over to our table and Ronnie greeted him with: 'Where the fuck have you been? You were supposed to be here early to talk to these two,' indicating us.

'I had to see someone,' Reggie muttered. Then he called the barman to fetch some more drinks.

At the same time the door opened and two men walked into the pub. As they approached a table to sit down, Pat was on his feet making signs to the twins that the two men were the law. They sat not far from where we were sitting, and Reggie shouted for the barman to give them a drink. It didn't seem to worry them that every so often a couple of cops showed up in the various pubs that they used.

'They are from the nick in Lime Street,' Reggie said.

After we had all got our drinks, the two police officers shouted over: 'Cheers for the drink, Reg.'

Ronnie put his glass up to his lips and said, 'Cheers.' Then he muttered 'Pigs.' He called over to the young man who was still sitting at the bar on his own. 'Are you all right, David?' The boy nodded. With a weird smile on his face Ronnie said, 'What do you think of him?' We just smiled back but we made no comment.

The pub started filling up with more members of the firm and I noticed that the two cops had quietly left. The talk became general and then Ian and I were left alone while the 'firm' talked 'business'. Getting involved was a very slow process. At this stage we were just drinking with them.

It was about two weeks later that we met the twins' older brother, Charles. He was slightly taller than the twins and very smartly dressed when he came into the pub one evening with his wife. I noticed that she stayed at the far end of the bar, but Charlie came over to Ronnie and Reggie, who were again sitting at the meeting table. We were introduced to him by Reggie and he seemed to be a very friendly type of man. 'What are you drinking?' he asked, looking first at Ian and then at me. Charlie was not, as far as we could tell, involved in the firm. He told us he had his own business in the clothing trade.

It seemed to us as though everybody had plenty of money. Every night was a party night, and money kept coming out of pockets as though it was burning a hole in them. Just a few weeks ago Ian and myself had been working hard each week for what it seemed each and every one of them was spending on drink every night. No matter how hard we worked, our money was peanuts compared to what we saw the firm handling.

On one such night, Ronnie called Ian over and asked him to go to the Gents cloakroom with him. Everybody looked up from their drinks to see where they were going, because that was where he took someone for a private talk or argument, and any of the firm who were in the bar suddenly went quiet. Ian looked apprehensive as he left me and walked over to the Gents. I wondered if something had gone wrong. To my relief, a few minutes later they came out joking with each other.

Ian walked over to me and said: 'Ronnie has just given me a oner [£100]. He wants me to go get a new suit.'

'What have you got to do for him?' I asked.

'Nothing! He just wants me to look a bit smart and be with him all the time.'

By now we had left our previous jobs and had found ourselves furnished flats. Things had been easy so far. We were getting money handed out regularly to us from Ronnie – he was more inclined to do that than Reggie. But we were doing nothing for it. But that £100 new suit was to cost Ian dearly. He had always been a very quiet person and had never ever got into any trouble. He had been a seaman like his uncles before him. Suddenly he was Ronnie Kray's right-hand man: from now on he had to accompany Ronnie whenever he went to important meetings. This arrangement was not popular with all of the firm. After all, he was still a stranger to most of them. Later I found out that Ronnie enjoyed playing one against the other and for this reason he was always changing his right-hand man as the mood took him.

Weeks passed and we were now members (by which I mean we were paid wages – which varied from week to week) of the best-known gang in London. Surprisingly perhaps the firm consisted of a hardcore of only about twenty men. There were many more on the fringe but they weren't really involved. People were led to believe that the firm could call on numerous men. I can tell you that wasn't really true.

One evening when I was in the club playing cards,

Billy came over to me and said: 'Reggie wants to see you round at the house.'

'OK,' I said, and left straight away.

When I got to the house in Vallance Road, where the twins' parents lived, Reggie said, 'How would you like a new set of wheels? We have two cars that have just arrived at one of our car showrooms in Walthamstow.'

He arranged for another member of the firm to drive us over to the showroom and it was about 7.30 when we got there. A man came over to us, whom I took to be the manager. 'Hello, Reggie. What can I do for you?'

'I have been told that you have got two new cars from Canada,' Reggie answered.

'That's right,' the man replied, 'but they are sold. They are being picked up tomorrow.'

'Too fucking bad,' said Reggie. 'We want them and we want them now. It's about time you did us a favour, you have done nothing for us for a long time.'

The man was starting to look worried. 'They have cost me a lot of money,' he complained. 'If you take them, I will be out of pocket. Can't you take one of the cars that are on the front?'

'No,' snapped Reggie. 'I want the ones that I came over for.'

Reggie and the poor, scared-looking man went into the office. I could hear heated exchanges coming from it and Reggie came out in ten minutes with the two sets of car keys. It wasn't too long before I found out that the firm had nothing to do with the car showroom at all, they just collected protection money from the owner. It was one of the many places that their weekly income was coming from.

Then the three of us each drove a car back to Vallance Road. When Ronnie came out to have a look at them he said to me: 'You'd better keep the one you are driving, and take me and Ian around in it.'

I thought to myself: 'Great, a brand new car just to drive him about in.' But from that moment on I was like a doctor on call twenty-four hours a day, for although Ronnie had picked Ian as his right-hand man of the moment Ian could not drive.

We were now really in a gangsters' world, and if we had wanted to get out, we should have done so before, because we definitely had no chance now. We were two small cogs in a big wheel, and it soon got around the East End that Ronnie and Reggie had got themselves two hard men from Scotland to back them up. I sensed this immediately when people's attitudes changed from being relaxed and friendly to being respectful because they knew I was now a member of the firm. I would rather they had just stayed friendly.

The two cars didn't last long. Reggie had only had his car about three days when he went up to the West End on a drinking spree. Coming back he wrapped it round a lamppost. He and his two companions just got out and walked away. That was the end of one car. I knew it wouldn't be too long before he wanted the other car and, sure enough, he took the other car away from me and the same thing happened. After that, I decided to buy my own car.

Shortly after then money started to get tight. Suddenly it seemed as if the firm could no longer afford to throw it around as they usually did. In the normal way, members of the firm were sent to the gaming clubs to collect protection money the clubs paid on the understanding that they would not get trouble from outsiders.

One evening there was a meeting called in one of the pubs that we frequented. We were told that there were too many people on the firm doing nothing, or getting money and not declaring it to the rest of the firm. We decided that evening, amongst ourselves, that it was about time we looked up some of the small-time crooks who were doing well, see whether we could 'blag' (by which I mean take but not steal) some cash off them. These 'crooks' were men who made a living out of stealing and paid the firm to leave them alone.

Ronnie also told us that he would be setting up a big deal in the next few days but he said he wouldn't be telling us anything about it yet. 'If it does come off,' he said confidentially, 'we will be made.' Then he added: 'Be careful. I have heard that the "Old Bill" have been making enquiries about us.'

CHAPTER 3

THE TANGIERS AFFAIR

Most of us were loyal to the twins, mainly through fear of ending up on a marble slab, which is why we went on various assignments for them without question. One such assignment started for me only a couple of nights after we had the pep talk about getting more money in – Ronnie's 'big deal'.

One evening I was in the club as usual when the phone rang. The manager answered, and was only on it for about a minute. Then he put the receiver down and came over to me and whispered: 'Ronnie wants you round at the house right away.'

I played out my hand and got up from the table. 'Sorry, mates,' I said, 'but I've got to go.'

I put on my jacket, and I reckon they all must have

known who had phoned. On my way out I told the manager: 'If Ian comes in, tell him to wait, I will be back later.'

When I got to Vallance Road, where Ronnie lived most of the time, he told me that we were going to the West End on some business. Had it been anyone but him, I would have asked what part of the West End and what for, but it was better to keep quiet until he was ready to tell me. So I drove to my flat and got into a suit, shirt and tie, and was back within the hour. I tooted the car horn and Ronnie came out of the house, immaculately dressed. As he got into the car he said: 'Make for Hyde Park.' Then, as we drove away, he said: 'We have a meeting with an American. His name is Alan, but we call him the Yank.'

It seemed that he had already been of great service to the firm in the past, by supplying them with guns. As we approached Hyde Park Corner Ronnie repeated what he had said to the firm a few days before about being on a good earner. I drove in silence thinking to myself: 'How many times have I heard that? He talks about these big deals and nothing materializes.'

He also told me to keep my mouth shut because none of the firm was to know about this meeting – which wasn't at all unusual. Then he told me to park the car round the back of the hotel. When we got out of the car we instinctively looked around us to make sure that we were not being followed by 'Old Bill'.

We walked into the foyer of the Hilton Hotel, which was teeming with activity, probably due to the fact there was a private boxing match on that evening. The Yank was already there waiting for us. He was a rather small man, aged about thirty-five, also smartly dressed. He led us up a short, wide staircase to the first floor and into a cocktail lounge, where he made for a table in a far corner which was very secluded. Before anything was said, he beckoned to the waiter and ordered drinks. Then he put forward the proposition.

The general idea was that he would go to Tangiers to have a meeting with three important black Africans from the Congo. They would part with a large sum of money, as a down payment to the firm to supply men and arms needed in order to get a high-ranking official freed from detention. The Yank then opened his briefcase and showed us various sketches of the different types of armoury they required, and he said very convincingly that he could pull off a big con and earn a lot of money. All he wanted to do was use the firm's name and take a cut of the down payment. 'You've got to hand it to him,' I thought. 'He is a real good talker.'

It seemed feasible enough and we were all for it, until he said that he would go to Tangiers in a few days' time on his own. He hadn't bargained for Ronnie's temper. Before he gave the Yank any answer, Ronnie called the waiter over to set up more drinks. Then he looked all around the bar, making sure that there were no police or photographers about. Then he exploded.

'Not fucking likely,' he said, staring right at the Yank, 'I will send someone with you from the firm.' His voice started to rise: 'How do we know that you won't use our good name to set them up, get the money and disappear?'

'Christ! You should know me by now,' the Yank replied. 'I have done a lot for you in the past, and we have always done all right.' He paused for a moment, then had a thought. 'What if I take someone with me? He could look after your interests. You can trust me on this one. There should be plenty in it for everybody.'

He suggested taking one of his own men with him.

Ronnie laughed sarcastically. 'You have got to be joking,' he said. 'He could go back to the States with you.'

The Yank didn't know what to say next. We just sat looking at each other and Ronnie kept looking round the bar. He beckoned the waiter over. 'Same again please.' I could see he was getting very uptight, and when he was in this frame of mind he was very difficult to talk to.

'I have a better idea,' he said suddenly. Before he told us what it was, he asked me if I had my passport handy.

'Yes,' I replied, 'it is at home.'

The Yank opened his mouth to say something.

'Just hang on a minute before you speak,' said Ronnie, 'this is my plan.' He pointed to me. 'He will be going with you.'

How the hell was I going to get out of going to Tangiers with the Yank? He was a bit too devious for me, and if he did double-cross the firm, he would just disappear and I would be left to face the music. However, I knew that there was no way I could get out of it. The Yank had no option, either, but to agree to our terms. By this time he could see that he couldn't argue with Ronnie when his mind was made up. He was a gun exporter and he had a large office near to where MI5's offices are situated, and he was no fool.

However, it was obvious to me that he wasn't very satisfied with these arrangements when it was left to us to make our plans for the trip. While we did this, Ronnie went through his usual routine of ordering more drinks and looking round the cocktail lounge suspiciously over his glasses. It was about ten o'clock before our arrangements were all completed and we got up to leave.

When we were driving back to the East End, Ronnie said: 'Don't let that bastard out of your sight. It all sounds good but I am not one hundred per cent sure of him. Don't let anyone on the firm know you are going abroad. Don't even tell Ian, at the moment this is between us, the Yank and yourself.'

The firm had changed its meeting-place to another pub, The Lion in Tapp Street, Bethnal Green. We used to call it Marge's or the widow's pub, after the landlady whom we all got on well with. She was a lovely lady: a slim and tall redhead in her early fifties and always very well dressed. She was like a second mother to the twins. The pub was just round the corner from the house in Vallance Road. When we arrived we could see by the number of cars outside that the firm was there, even though it was just after closing time. This was nothing unusual. When we walked in, everybody looked at us and I thought to myself : 'I bet they have all been wondering where we have been.' We went straight upstairs without speaking to any of them and walked into one of the private rooms where we had meetings.

Reggie had followed us up. 'Well! How did you get on with him?'

It was common knowledge that Reggie did not care much for the Yank. He was always very suspicious of him, and was often heard to say that he thought he was working for the police.

The three of us talked about the meeting that had taken place that evening in the hotel when, out of the blue Ronnie started shouting at Reggie: 'Here's me trying to do a deal and get some money for the firm, but all you do is drink and criticize everything I try to do!'

The twins seemed to spend a lot of time arguing but I noticed it was normally Ronnie who took the lead. He took the lead in everything to do with the firm. He really did have the ability to command and once he had made up his mind to do something he was not to be deterred – unlike Reggie, who could normally be talked out of things.

Ronnie was silent for a minute, and I butted in: 'You'd better keep your voices down or you will have Marge coming up wondering what all the noise is about.'

As I spoke, there was a tap on the door. I opened it and Marge, the landlady, was standing there. She asked me if we would like any drinks sent up and told me that the men in the bar downstairs could hear us. She was a very nice woman and let us have the run of the pub allowing us to drink in a private room after hours.

Things had now quietened down and Reggie turned to me and asked if everything had gone off all right at the meeting.

'It all looks very interesting to me,' I commented. 'The Yank seems to know what he is talking about. Ronnie wants me to go to Tangiers too.'

Reggie told me to be very careful of the Yank. 'You will need some readies,' he said.

Ronnie got up off his seat and, putting his arm around my shoulder, said: 'Go and see Fat Wally at the club and tell him I said you needed expense money.'

I nodded in agreement and left them to talk while I went downstairs to have a quick drink before I left to see Fat Wally. Ian bought one for me and everybody wanted to know what the shouting had been about upstairs. None of them would have dared to come up and interfere when there were arguments.

Time was getting on – it was about midnight. I whispered to Ian: 'I have got to go. I can't tell you anything, but I will see you in a few days' time.'

I shouted goodnight and walked out of the pub

and drove to the club where Wally worked. As I drove the short distance, Reggie's last words to me were still ringing in my ears. 'Look after yourself in Tangiers and make sure the Yank doesn't drop you in it.'

For the next few days I stayed away from the firm, mainly because I didn't want to be questioned about where I was going. On the Wednesday morning I went to the Yank's house in Bayswater, where I had previously arranged to meet him. He lived in a big, imposing-looking house and he invited me in while he phoned for a taxi. He asked me how long I had been with the firm, but I was in no mood for his questions, remembering what Reggie had said. The taxi then arrived to take us straight to Heathrow Airport. On the way, he suggested that we get on the plane separately, and he said we should not communicate with each other until we got to Gibraltar. I thought to myself: 'What's all this cloak-and-dagger stuff in aid of?'

When we touched down at Gibraltar, we got a taxi to take us to a hotel facing the seafront. It was a very cheap and dingy-looking building with about forty bedrooms, but it was very busy. We settled in and I said: 'I'm going to have a drink. I will see you at breakfast.'

I had the evening to myself and as I roamed about my mind went back to the last time I was there – when I was in the Marines on a ship going to Korea. It was back in the fifties. We had docked at Gibraltar, and some of us had been given shore leave. A crowd of us went to a local nightspot called the Trocodero. We had the usual serviceman's set-to with the local lads and I remembered the captain reading out a telegram that the mayor had sent to the ship. It said: 'If the Marines fight as well in Korea as they did in my town last night, the war will be over quickly.'

The next morning I woke up with a lousy headache after the night before when I'd been on drink. We met for breakfast as planned and the Yank told me he had spent the evening in his room reading. After breakfast we made our way to the docks and boarded a ferry to Tangiers. When we arrived, we were met by a tall, thin man with a moustache. I was surprised to see him because I had not been told that we would be met by anybody. It seemed to me that the Yank knew him pretty well.

'Who's he?' I asked the Yank. 'And who does he work for?'

'He's all right,' he answered, 'he will be acting as my interpreter.'

The man took us to another part of the docks and asked us to wait at the quayside. He said he would be back soon and we watched him go on board a yacht which was moored there. After a while, he came off the yacht and we were asked to accompany him on board for a meeting with the same three African officials. By this stage I was feeling very unsure of them, and I was definitely not getting on the yacht. I thought to myself: 'If this is a con, I want my two feet on dry land. If they were to get suspicious while we were at sea, we'd have no chance.'

I said to the Yank: 'I don't think we should go on board. We were supposed to have the meeting at one of the hotels here.'

Thankfully, the Yank agreed to what I had just said. He explained to the other man that we both thought it would be better to have the meeting at a hotel on the seafront. We made our way back to the hotel, not knowing whether or not they would agree to come. After a few minutes they arrived with the interpreter.

We all sat down in a corner of the bar and had a few drinks. One of the men asked us what the plan was to get the high-ranking person out of detention. I got a strong feeling that the Yank had already had talks with them before this meeting. Looking and listening to them, in my mind I felt that they were not strangers to each other.

The Yank then discussed with them how it could be arranged for some men to come from London and free this person. He made it sound very easy. I just sat back and observed what was being said. Then he picked up his briefcase, which was on the floor beside him, put it on the table and opened it. He took out some papers and handed them to one of the men.

'These are the type of guns that I can supply you with, they would be right for your purpose,' he said. 'We can also arrange for men to come over with them to help you with your cause. You can have them at your disposal any time. We have also got a helicopter standing by, and a pilot who is willing to do this mission for a substantial fee.'

Just then, one of the Africans said something in his own language to the interpreter, who turned to the Yank and said: 'They want to know what the down payment would be.'

After the figure of £75,000 was mentioned, the three Africans started talking among themselves in their own language.

'What about the twins?' one of them asked. 'Will they be coming too?'

'Of course they will,' answered the Yank, 'assuming we can make a deal. The plan would not work without them.'

I did believe at this point that the Yank, who had done all the talking, really thought that they would part with the cash. Then one of the men said that there would be a prepayment when they could see that the helicopter was in Gibraltar. Now I definitely knew that this was one of the many plans to con someone out of their money, for we had no access to any helicopters.

The Yank said: 'That will be all right, I can arrange for it to be there whenever you like.'

They then asked for one of the twins to come on the next meeting and a date was made for two weeks later. I knew that the request for one of the twins to go on the next trip was impossible.

We all stood up and shook hands. The Yank and I left the hotel first and the interpreter followed. As we walked to the dock to get a hovercraft back to Gibraltar, he said to us: 'Well, it didn't work. I am sure they didn't believe that you could do all the things you said you could. I don't think you convinced them – I will have to get out of Tangiers now in case they find out I was working with you.'

We shook hands and said goodbye. The two of us made our way back to Gibraltar on the hovercraft.

I said to the Yank: 'I've got a feeling that you're pulling a con. Now I know why Ronnie wanted me here.'

He only made one comment: 'The twins will be very disappointed. But I can only tell them I tried.'

When we landed back in Gibraltar he said: 'I will see you back at the hotel. There are a few things I want to do before we catch the plane back to England.'

'All right,' I replied.

Then I made my way back to the hotel to pack my bag. My orders had been not to let him out of my sight – it could have been a double-cross but there was nothing I could do about it. I knew he couldn't leave the country without me; he would have been too scared of what would happen when he got back to London. I just hoped that Ronnie wouldn't find out.

We nearly missed the plane because the Yank was late getting back to the hotel, and when we got to the airport we went through the same routine of sitting apart and not communicating with each other. When we landed at Heathrow I made a phone call and just said: 'I'm back.'

We got a taxi to Bayswater and I asked him if he had a message for the twins. He just said he would be in touch. I then made my way back to

Vallance Road. Some of the firm were there and I was taken upstairs.

'Well,' said Reggie. 'How did you get on? Did the Yank get any money?'

I had to tell him that nothing had been handed over and he was never out of my sight.

'Are you sure?' they said.

'Yes,' I replied. 'Nothing was handed over.'

Reggie started shouting. 'I told you that fucking Yank was no good. He has never done a good deal for us yet. I don't know why the fuck you trust him.'

It was now my turn to be nervous. If they ever found out that the Yank was on his own for a few hours, things would be very bad for me. But that was the end as far as I was concerned. The big con that never came off. Whether or not the Yank completed the con, we never found out.

CHAPTER 4

THE CORNELL SHOOTING

One evening we were all summoned to a meeting in Marge's pub, The Lion. There were two bars there, one of which was frequented by local police. They would be on one side and we would be on the other. Ronnie always told Marge to give them a drink.

He had been drinking very heavily by the time we arrived. Ian and I were the first to walk in, and Ronnie got us a drink. A few seconds later Reggie walked in with two more members of the firm. He didn't look pleased, and went straight over to where Ronnie was standing by the bar.

'What do you want everybody here for?' he demanded.

'I am having a party, that's why,' Ronnie answered.

Nothing more was said. As I stood there I thought to myself : 'Christ, he has started early, it's only seven o'clock.'

By this time the pub was starting to fill up with people, who were mostly strangers to me. Ronnie went over to a couple of them and put his arm round their shoulders and whispered something to them. He then called out to the bar in general that he was going somewhere else for a drink, and he told them to stay where they were until he got back. We all looked at each other. Ronnie seemed drunk but it was unusual for him to act so aggressively so early in the evening.

'Who's got a car with them?' Ronnie called out. In fact, only about three or four members knew how to drive.

When nobody answered he called out for Connie, another member of the firm – a married man who collected protection money. 'Ain't that bastard here yet?' he shouted. 'He's always late getting here when I want him – he's always poncing around with other bastards.'

Then he called out to me: 'Have you got your car parked outside?'

Very reluctantly I said, 'Yes.' There was no point my arguing with him. He was the Al Capone of

London and he knew it. When he snapped his fingers everybody jumped.

While all this was going on, Reggie was still in the room upstairs but he came down into the bar and Ronnie went over to him and whispered something. He didn't say where he was going to anybody else in the pub, but he started walking to the door so I followed him to get the car.

He turned around at the door and shouted over to Ian, who was standing at the bar talking, 'You'd better come with me, you can keep me company.'

When we were settled in the car, I asked him where he wanted me to take him.

'Drive round to Vallance Road,' he answered.

When we got there, he got out of the car rather unsteadily. 'Wait here a minute,' he told us.

He went into the house and I said to Ian: 'He is in a fucking bad mood tonight. Where does he want us to go?'

'I don't know,' said Ian. 'You know he never tells anybody anything.'

Ronnie then came out of the house and got back into the car.

Before I started the engine I said: 'Where do you want me to take you?'

'Take me to the Blind Beggar,' he replied.

'Where's that?' I asked. It wasn't one of the pubs we normally frequented.

'Drive up to Whitechapel and turn left at the lights, then go up to the next set of lights and go straight over.'

When we got over the lights, he made me do a U-turn to go back again. Then he said: 'When you go over the lights stop at the bank on the corner.'

By doing this we had passed the pub once and now approached it from the opposite direction. I parked the car outside the bank, opposite the Blind Beggar pub.

I asked him what time he wanted me to pick him up, assuming that he was going to drink in that pub all evening.

'I want you to stay here!' he said aggressively. 'I shall only be a short time.'

I told him that I might have to pull away from there as it was still early evening and the traffic on the main road was very heavy. He scowled and kept complaining that nobody was loyal to him.

Just before he got out of the car, he handed a small object, which looked like a gun, to Ian. 'Keep that in your pocket,' he told him, 'just in case I need it.'

It wasn't at all unusual for him to hand over a gun

to one of the firm to carry for him. He always said that one day there would be someone wanting to shoot him, and he wanted to be prepared. But Ian's face turned white. As far as I knew he had never held a gun before. As they walked across the road to the pub, I settled down in the car prepared for a long wait. I knew from experience that Ronnie's five minutes could be anything up to an hour. But this time I was wrong. Within five minutes they were out of the pub and walking back to the car. They both got in the back seat and I was told to take them to Marge's pub.

'That was a quick visit,' I thought to myself. As I was driving back the whole area of Whitechapel came alive with the sounds of police sirens blaring, and several police cars passed me at top speed. Ronnie leaned over from the back of the car and, with his hand on my shoulder, said, 'There must have been an accident.' He then started to laugh loudly.

I looked at them both in my mirror. Ian sat there like a stone. He was just staring out of the window and he did not speak a word. I felt at that moment that something was very wrong – they were both acting so strangely. Ian's face was as white as a sheet and Ronnie kept laughing and talking to himself, repeating over and over again: 'I have done it at last, I have done it!'

I was much too concerned about Ian to ask what had happened. So I kept quiet and just drove back to the pub. When I pulled up outside, we all got out of the car without a word. Ronnie rushed right into the pub and hurried upstairs to one of the rooms without speaking to anybody, and Ian and I walked over to the bar and had a couple of drinks.

I whispered to him: 'What happened back there?'

I could see he was in a state of shock. He either couldn't or wouldn't tell me what had happened in the Blind Beggar.

There must have been about thirty or forty people in our bar. I did not know half of them, but I noticed there were a couple of the local police in the other bar.

Before Reggie went upstairs he came over to where Ian and myself were standing. 'Where did you take him?' he asked. He was looking very worried.

'To the Blind Beggar,' I answered.

'Who was in there?' he asked.

'I don't know,' I replied. 'He told me to stay outside.'

Then he turned to Ian: 'What happened?'

Ian took him to one side and whispered something to him. I sensed that there was something wrong because Reggie looked flustered and ran upstairs.

While they were upstairs somebody came into the bar and shouted excitedly: 'There has been a shooting in Whitechapel Road!'

At that moment the people who had been summoned to the pub for a party must have put two and two together, because they left the pub very discreetly and very quickly. By this time, after a couple of drinks, Ian had got a bit of colour back in his face and he told me that Ronnie had shot someone in the pub that evening.

'Did you shoot anybody?' I asked Ian.

'Of course I didn't,' he answered. 'I just fired the gun in the air, the one he gave me in the car.'

'Did he also have a gun?'

'Yes,' he replied.

'Do yourself a favour,' I told him, 'and go home. I will come over to your place later.'

He shook his head and said, 'I can't.'

Just then Reggie came downstairs. He looked around to see how many had left the bar. He could see that the pub had emptied and by the look on his face I could see that he wasn't pleased. He looked over to the other bar where the local police often drank, but they had gone. He told those of the firm who were still in the bar that Ronnie had shot Cornell. What happened to Cornell could have happened to anybody that night. I did not know the man personally, but others on the firm sometimes had drinks with him. Although he was based in the East End, he was a friend of the Richardson gang, rival villains from South London. About a couple of days earlier, Ronnie had been told that Cornell had been going round making snide remarks about him behind his back. 'A fat pouf' was one of the things he'd been calling him.

When Ronnie came down, he saw that his so-called friends, whom he had invited to a party, had all gone, but he was composed by now and fully in control again. I looked at him and thought, 'How could he be so calm after just shooting someone?'

He called over a man named Charlie and handed him a carrier-bag. 'Take that out and get rid of it. Don't come back here – just go straight home and we will be in touch.'

Charlie was out of the pub in a flash.

The remainder of the firm were told to go to a pub in the High Street in Stoke Newington called the Coach and Horses. This was another one of the firm's meeting-places. The pub was quite a large one and managed by a very nice friend of mine, whom we used to call Blondy Bill and who didn't like the idea of the firm using his place for meetings but, like everyone else, had no option; quite simply, he didn't want any trouble.

On our way over to the pub I said to Ian: 'Now you are in trouble. You have been with Ronnie and he has shot someone. He may even have killed him. What fucking chance have you got to get out of this? If he goes down, you will go down with him. If I was you I'd have it away – you know you will get no help from anybody.'

Ian made no comment. I think he was still too shocked at what had taken place.

When we arrived at the pub plans were already being put in motion to hide Ronnie. Nobody seemed to care about Ian. I could see he was out in the cold after being involved with a shooting done by somebody else. That night Ronnie went into hiding. He was taken to one of the many hide-outs that were available for any emergencies. Now Reggie was in charge.

The next meeting was in the house of a friend of the firm's in Walthamstow. It was over all the newspapers that there had been a shooting and by then most of the people who lived in the East End had guessed that Ronnie had shot Cornell. The firm were feeling very uneasy and talked amongst themselves about what had happened at the Blind

Beggar. They thought it was only a matter of time before Ronnie got arrested. A few of them decided that they had had enough of this way of life and took the opportunity of getting out during all the commotion. With Reggie worrying about his brother he never paid much attention to what every member of the firm was doing. I stayed put because of my concern for Ian.

The remaining members of the firm kept in touch with each other, and messages were carried backwards and forwards between the hide-out and the pub where we drank. One evening I was told to get hold of Ian as I was the only one who knew where he lived and had promised him I would tell no one. He lived with his girlfriend, but the twins were worried that if he was seen, he would be picked up by the police. This was something they had to avoid, for Ronnie's protection.

I drove over to his flat in North London and knocked on his door. It seemed a long time before anybody answered. I saw the curtain move and then the door was opened by Ian. I followed him up the stairs.

'You are wanted,' I said. 'I have got to take you over to Walthamstow because they want you to go away, out of London for a few days.'

Ian was a bit apprehensive. 'Wouldn't it be better

if I stay where I am? You're the only one who knows where I live.'

I thought for a moment, then I suggested: 'If you don't want to go, I will go back and tell them that I can't find you.'

'No,' he replied, 'I had better come with you. They will see me all right.'

I looked at him. 'I think you had better be on your guard at all times. Just remember that you are an eyewitness against them and don't forget the old saying, "Blood is thicker than water". If you don't want to go I am quite prepared to drive you up to Scotland until Ronnie gets nicked.'

'Don't worry,' Ian replied. 'If I think that anything is going to happen, I will get out quick.'

We got in the car and I dropped him off outside the hide-out. As he got out of the car I said, 'Don't forget what I have told you.'

A few days passed and I heard nothing from Ian, so I went round to see his girlfriend. She was very upset and crying. 'Where's Ian? I haven't seen him for two days. He hasn't been back since he left a note saying he had gone somewhere with you.'

'Are you sure he hasn't been in touch?' I asked.

'Yes,' she answered, 'I wouldn't be here crying if I knew where he was.'

I tried to reassure her, then I left, saying I would be in touch. I drove over to the house in Vallance Road, where Reggie was holding his meetings.

'Where is Ian?' I asked him. 'I have just left his girlfriend. She is very worried and doesn't know where he is. She might go to the police. She loves him – we had better give her some kind of reassurance.'

Reggie nodded. 'You know we are trying to keep this as quiet as possible. We've managed to get them both out of the country for a few days.'

I got a feeling that he didn't completely trust me because he knew that Ian and I were close friends. He told me that he and Ronnie were on their way to the villa of an old-time gangster friend of theirs abroad. He added that Ian had left a message for his girlfriend and that he would be back in a few days' time.

Nothing went right while they were in hiding. The firm could not get their hands on any money – it seemed as though everybody had decided to stay away from the clubs, and money was tight. The managers just kept making excuses. We all kept away from Vallance Road, too, on orders from Reggie, although he did arrange for two of the lesser members of the firm to stay there – one of whom was a married man with a family, who objected to this, but he had no option but to go.

Somebody got in touch with Reggie through the East End grapevine and told him that the barmaid from the Blind Beggar could be a threat to Ronnie. He sent a message to the manager and asked him to meet him at another meeting place. The manager was very reluctant to meet him, but he was persuaded.

Reggie told him that he was sorry about what had happened in his pub. He asked if the barmaid was all right. The manager said: 'She will keep her mouth shut. The police interviewed her and she didn't tell them anything.'

Reggie looked relieved. 'Tell her to keep it that way. There will be a few quid sent round to her if she keeps to what she has already told the police.'

We waited, thinking that Ronnie would be arrested at any time, but nothing happened.

When Ronnie came back to the East End his position was even stronger and he really became 'The Godfather'. He started to make himself busy again, and called a meeting.

'Nothing has been done all the time I've been away,' he said, in true Al Capone style. 'The Cornell thing is finished, no bastard will do me for it now.'

However, they did find out later that there were two more witnesses to the shooting; they were two businessmen who called in at the pub on their way to play cards. They were warned off by the firm. Time passed and we all started to forget about the shooting. I felt, though, that the police must be building up a dossier on our activities because the local officers were not around drinking in the pubs as much as before. Perhaps they had been told to keep a low profile to prevent the firm getting wise to the fact that the Regional Crime Squad was interested in them.

CHAPTER 5

NOBBY SCAPEGOAT

Now that the Cornell shooting was forgotten, at least as far as the firm was concerned, and now that Ronnie was fully back in control, a lot of club owners who had not paid their dues when he was in hiding were now too scared to refuse. They realized that the firm was led by two of the most ruthless gangsters in London, who never ever forgot anybody who managed to break away.

One man who did break away, paid a price. He left the firm and started his own business quite successfully. We knew him as Nobby. He was always smartly dressed and smoked big cigars and he never came in contact with the firm unless he was sent for. He was a very good friend of 'big brother Charlie'.

The firm summoned him one evening. 'We need some readies,' he was told. 'We have been checking up on you and we know that you have been doing very well lately. We haven't bothered to ask you before, but now is the time to prove your friendship.'

He was another one of the many who were wary of the twins and it showed on his face. He told them that 'things were bad' and he had 'no cash to spare', but he had a warehouse full of different types of merchandise that would fetch quite a lot of money into the firm if it could arrange for transport to pick it up. The warehouse was in Kent.

I felt sorry for him. Here was a man who was handing over his stock and could do nothing about it. I knew that he would not dare to go to the police, even if he wanted to – he had a wife and children and he was scared of what might happen.

In the days that followed we had to find out if any of the small-time crooks that we could trust had a large van and wanted to earn some ready cash. That was easy, there was one man who always wanted to work for the firm. He was a loner, a bit of a drunk and an occasional drug-user. He was also a small-time crook who had served time in prison and he would be more than willing to do something in order to be one of the firm. His name was Jack McVitie but we all knew him as Jack the Hat. He got the name through always wearing a hat – he was never seen without one.

I was sent to a club in Dalston, North London, run by four brothers. 'Is Jack the Hat in tonight?' I asked when I went into the foyer.

One of the brothers said, 'Yes, he is fucking drunk as usual. He is downstairs.'

I made my way down to the basement bar to see him and told him that the twins wanted him to do a favour. 'It could be a good earner for you. If you are interested I will pick you up tomorrow night and take you to the pub and they will tell you what they want you to do.'

He agreed, and I said: 'I will pick you up at about six-thirty. Make sure you are sober.'

I picked him up at his house in Forest Road, East London, as arranged. I drove him to where he had to meet the firm and when we walked into the pub he got so excited that they had actually sent for him to do a job for them. He was asked if he could get a van and take it to Kent to pick up some merchandise from a warehouse.

'Yeah! Yeah! Of course I can,' he said eagerly. 'What's in it for me?'

'We will pay you £200 to pick it up. Here's fifty

for expenses – you will get the rest when the job is done,' they told him. He was handed a piece of paper with the address of where he had to deliver the goods on it.

After all the talking was done and the arrangements made, he wanted to stay in our company, but nobody wanted him to because he was such a bigmouth and most of us knew he couldn't care less whom he insulted. I managed to get him to leave with me and I dropped him off at one of his favourite haunts.

I went back and Ronnie called me over to one side. 'I don't trust him,' he said.

'Well, he is the only one you can get to do it on such short notice,' I replied.

'I know. That's why I want you to follow him in your car,' he said. 'Just to make sure he picks up and delivers.'

I went home early that night because Jack the Hat was going to leave at five in the morning. I followed him to Kent and sat in my car, unseen by Jack, until he loaded up. Then he made his way back and I drove a short distance behind him. But he knew my car and he must have got suspicious because he drove so fast he made sure he lost me in the traffic. I made my way back to London and went to the twins' house where

I told them that I had lost him. Ronnie almost exploded. 'The bastard has double-crossed us. Who the fuck said we could trust him?'

I tried to calm him down. 'Maybe he has already gone to unload the van at the address you gave him.'

Ronnie turned to a couple of the firm who were there. 'Go round to this address,' he told them, handing them a slip of paper, 'and see whether he has delivered the goods. If he hasn't been there, don't come back until you find out where he is.'

After an hour passed they came back. 'He has been there,' they said, 'but some of the gear was missing.'

Much later we were told through the grapevine that Jack had stopped off somewhere on the way back to London and sold some of the goods. He never came back for his £200.

Poor Jack the Hat. That was one bad mistake he should never have made. No one ever double-crossed the firm and got away with it. I think we all knew it would only be a matter of time before they did something about it. There was some talk of shooting him in the legs in case it got around how easy it was to double-cross the firm. But they soon stopped looking for Jack the Hat because they knew it wouldn't be too long before he turned up. He was such an idiot. He kept going round the clubs telling people that he had turned the Kray gang over and that they didn't do anything about it.

Soon after this the twins decided to throw a party one evening. It went on into the night and Reggie drank heavily. He got fed up with hearing his brother boasting about the murder of Cornell, that he now assumed he had got away with. All of a sudden Reggie changed the conversation. He said he thought that Nobby had arranged with Jack the Hat to sell some of the gear before it got delivered and was part of the double-cross. I knew that wasn't true – Nobby was not the kind of man to do anything like that. There were other things on Reggie's mind but he was looking for a scapegoat. Nobby was going to be it.

Ronnie was geeing him up: 'Get out and do something to someone,' he said, and Reggie was getting more and more intoxicated. It looked as if we were all in for a bad night. One or two of the firm who were married made excuses to go home. Ronnie kept telling them to stay. No one had the guts to leave when he didn't want them to. They all knew he could and would shoot any one of us just to prove that he was in charge.

By about four in the morning we were all just sitting there. Ian asked Ronnie if he could leave. 'I haven't seen my bird for a few days,' he complained. 'Will you drive me home?' he asked me.

I jumped up off my chair – I was only too pleased to get out of the house – but Reggie looked up and interrupted.

'He'll drop you off,' he said, pointing to one of the firm. 'He's got to go home to his wife.'

My heart sank. 'Why can't I take him? I have got to go that way,' I said to Reggie.

'I may need you later,' he answered.

They both left and the relief was clear on their faces as they walked out of the door.

Reggie went into the hall. When he came back into the room he was holding a gun.

'What the hell are you going to do with that?' I asked, looking at him in amazement. He looked very agitated.

'That bastard keeps telling me that he is doing everything. I'll fucking show him.'

There was more screaming and crying from Reggie, which happened when he got in a rage. This was the sort of thing that we were all used to if they were fighting amongst themselves. Nobody would dare to interfere because they would turn on us if we did.

Reggie got on the phone and told the person who answered that he wanted to speak to Wally.

'Fetch your van over,' he told him, then he listened for a moment. 'I don't care if you're bloody busy, get someone else to look after the club.'

He banged the phone down on Fat Wally.

It took him about half an hour to get to the house. I opened the door.

'What does he want me for at this time of the morning?' he asked.

I felt so sorry for him – he was shaking like a leaf and he wasn't even a member of the firm.

'I don't know,' I answered. 'You had better ask him.'

Reggie asked Wally if he knew where Nobby lived. 'Yes, I think so,' he replied, not suspecting anything.

'I want you to drive me over there because I want to have a chat with him.'

Wally laughed nervously. 'What, at this time of the morning? He will be in bed. Can't he take you?' he asked, pointing to me. 'I am very busy in the club – I'm the only one looking after it.'

Reggie exploded. 'Who's fucking looking after it right now?' he screamed.

Wally tried to pacify him. 'I told the barman that I was only nipping out for half an hour and the barman said he couldn't handle it any longer than that.'

Ronnie sat through this tirade without saying a word, knowing full well what his brother had in mind.

It was now about five in the morning and I felt that something terrible was going to happen but I was powerless to do anything about it. Now that Wally was there, I said: 'I am going home to get some shuteye,' but Reggie stopped me in my tracks.

'Hang on a minute,' he said. 'I want you to come with me.'

Knowing that he had the gun, I said, 'You don't need me to have a chat with Nobby. Anyway, it's time we all got some sleep.'

Reggie told Wally to go outside and start the van up. Then he turned to me. 'Go out with him,' he said. 'I will be out in a minute.'

When I got outside in the street I said to Wally: 'What on earth made you tell him where Nobby lived? If you had said that you didn't know his address we wouldn't be going over there now.'

'What does he want to speak to him about at this time of the morning?' asked Wally.

'You ask him,' I replied.

Reggie came out of the house wearing a strange smile. 'I will drive,' he said, so Wally moved over into the passenger seat. 'You just tell me how to get to the house.'

It was very quiet on the streets at that time in the morning, all we passed were some early risers and milk-floats. When we got to the part of London that Nobby lived in, Wally told Reggie to drive down a cul-de-sac and pointed to a block of flats. 'He lives on the first floor,' Wally pointed upwards. 'The one with the blue curtains.'

Reggie turned the van so it faced outwards towards the main road. As he got out of the vehicle, Wally said: 'I'll wait for you here. I'm tired so I will have a kip, because I have been working all night.'

'You had better come with me,' said Reggie, 'you know what door it is.' He looked at me. 'You'd better come too.'

We all got out of the van and walked up the stairs to the first floor.

'Knock on the door,' he told Wally. 'He will come down and open the door if he hears your voice.'

It was then that Wally seemed to realize that he was being used, because he started to sweat. He knocked on the door very softly, but there was no answer. Reggie got impatient and banged hard on the door. After a few minutes a woman's voice called out: 'Who is it? Do you know what time it is?'

'It's Reggie, I want to speak to Nobby.'

She called back: 'He's in bed.'

'Tell him to get up,' Reggie said, 'it's important.'

Just then Nobby appeared shouting: 'I'm coming! I'm coming!'

He opened the door. 'What's wrong? What are you all doing here at this time in the morning? You could have phoned if you needed me for anything.'

Reggie's voice was quiet. 'There's nothing wrong, I just want to talk to you.'

We weren't invited in, and Reggie said: 'Tell your wife to go in the kitchen and make a cup of tea.'

The kitchen was situated near the front door so I followed her in. She whispered to me: 'What is he going to do? Is he going to harm my husband?'

I had only met Nobby's wife once before, and I thought that she was a very quiet and timid woman. Nobby never brought her to any of the parties that the firm had. I told her that Reggie was in a strange mood but I didn't think that he would harm his brother's best friend. I told her that I would go outside and see what was happening.

As I walked out of the kitchen to the front door I saw Reggie take the gun out of his pocket and point it at Nobby. Just a split second before he fired I pushed Nobby to the floor. He went down with a bang and his legs went up in the air. The bullet, which would probably have hit him in the chest, ended up in his foot.

Wally was so shocked by this unexpected turn of events, he disappeared down the stairs and into the van. I bent over Nobby and whispered: 'Stay where you are. I'll try to get him out.'

Just then his poor wife came running out of the kitchen. 'You bastard!' she screamed at Reggie. 'You have shot my husband!'

I shouted at Reggie that Nobby was badly hurt and he had better get out of there. I knew that my quick actions had saved Nobby's life that morning.

The shot must have been heard all over the building because lights were going on in the other flats. People were opening their doors and shutting them again. As we walked down the stairs we were seen by men who were leaving for work that day. Reggie was such a well-known face in the East End that he must have been recognized by somebody. Yet nobody phoned for the police. If they had, we would surely have been stopped. It was the same as the Cornell shooting – the East End wall of silence went up.

Reggie got into the back of the van and I got in next to Wally, who already had the engine running.

'You had better drive,' Reggie said. 'You know the way out of these flats.'

I could see that Wally was still very nervous: he was driving so fast, it was a miracle that he didn't get stopped for speeding. We could hear Reggie talking to himself but couldn't understand a word. Wally couldn't get back quick enough. We were both relieved when we pulled up at the house. It must have been about seven o'clock in the morning. Wally didn't want to go into the house.

'Can I go home now?' he asked.

To his relief Reggie said: 'Yes, go back to the club and keep your mouth shut!'

I thought to myself, poor Wally, now he was like me; involved with no way out.

Ronnie was in bed when we entered the house but he must have heard us drive up.

'Go and tell Ron that I have shot Nobby,' Reggie said to me.

At that moment Ronnie came into the room from his bedroom and heard what Reggie said.

'You fucking bastard!' he yelled. 'Now you have really got us into trouble!'

There was so much shouting going on between them that it is a wonder the police didn't come to see what the noise was all about. Ronnie then took charge, and got on the phone to big brother. Poor Charlie, the only time they called on him was when one of them was in trouble. I am sure he never knew half of what was going on.

'Get round here quick,' he told Charlie. There was a pause while Ronnie listened, then he said: 'Never mind what time it is,' and he hung up.

Charlie arrived shortly after and it seemed obvious to him which one of them was in trouble by the look on Reggie's face.

'He has shot your mate, Nobby,' Ronnie said. 'That bastard has really done it now.'

Charlie looked shocked. 'What the fuck did you shoot him for? He is a friend of mine.' He was shouting now, 'For what reason?'

'I don't have to tell you why I shot him,' Reggie answered.

Charlie looked at the three of us: 'Some bastard had better tell me,' he said.

He was pacing the floor, so I decided to butt in. 'He's not badly hurt,' I told him. 'He only got hit in the foot.' But I shouldn't have opened my mouth because it started Reggie off.

'It should have been his head. He might be your friend, but he's not mine!' he screamed.

Charlie was very annoyed and said: 'I have known Nobby for a long time. He has always been very loyal to us. I don't care what you do – just leave my friends alone. We had better stop all this arguing and see if the Doc can go round and patch him up.'

'The Doc' had a practice in the East End and he always came out if he was needed.

'By now the police could be there,' Ronnie said.

I spoke up. 'There must have been a lot of people who saw Reggie coming away from the flat.'

Charlie looked straight at me. 'Who took him round to Nobby's place?'

I answered, pointing at Reggie. 'He phoned Wally at the club and ordered him to come and pick him up.'

'Did you go with him?' he asked me.

'Yes,' I replied, 'I had no option – he was determined to see Nobby last night, or should I say this morning? Anyway, I'll leave you to it. I'm going home – you know where to get in touch with me.'

I was never told whether the police went round to Nobby, but I assumed they would never have known enough to investigate the matter. Only one good thing came out of all this: the twins never did bother Nobby again.

CHAPTER 6

OUTSIDE CONNECTIONS AND THREATS

There were some lighter moments in our lives. Parties were always popular with the firm – Reggie, in particular, loved a party. Often we would be in a pub, having a few pints accompanied by our wives and girlfriends, and somebody would shout: 'Let's have a party!'

Somebody else would reply: 'OK! Let's go to my place!'

If it wasn't someone's house it might be a private room in a club, like the Regency Club in Stoke Newington. We would have a whale of a time – eating, drinking and dancing till the small hours. No strangers were ever allowed upstairs at the club if we were having a get-together.

We never had parties in Vallance Road. The

twins' parents lived there of course and I suppose that made things more complicated. I knew both of them quite well: the twins' mother, Violet, was always very welcoming to the firm if we went round there individually and used to lay on plenty of tea and sandwiches (the twins loved their mother's cooking). She was a lovely woman and I liked her very much – as did all the firm. She was discreet, too, and always left the room if we were discussing the firm's business. It was obvious that the twins thought the world of her. They got on less well with their father Charles, however. He was a dealer in second-hand gold and, although I always found him a sociable sort of fellow (like Reggie in that respect) and enjoyed the occasional pint with him, the twins didn't see eye to eye with him.

In the way that everyone has a good side to their personality, the twins had one to theirs. It was not unusual, for example, to see Ronnie handing a couple of quid to elderly East Enders who had approached him in the pub saying they were short of cash. If the twins were asked for a donation to charity, they would give freely. They were especially generous to the clubs helping young up-and-coming boxers. Both of them had been keen boxers in their teenage days. In fact, Reggie was still a keep-fit fanatic and used to run regularly round the park next to the house in Vallance Road.

The firm were on very friendly terms with some great stars of the day like Diana Dors and some of the visiting stars from America. Of course, they all knew that we were gangsters, but it seemed to fascinate them being in our company. There was nothing in it for them really, apart from the fact they could say they had been wined and dined by the firm. The twins had entertained the great Judy Garland many times. She really got the red-carpet treatment, being taken to the smartest nightclubs in the West End. There was also a singer over here, singing in the popular nightspots. His name was Billy Daniels. We all arranged to go to Luton where he was appearing. We had a fabulous night. After his act he came and joined us at our table for the rest of the evening – the twins had met him many times before. Lots of well-known celebrities kept on coming up to speak to him, and I had the pleasure of driving him back to the Astor club, a London nightspot, to see a midnight cabaret and have a late meal.

Then there was George Raft, the film star. The firm were all fascinated by him. He was not only good looking and immaculately dressed, he was also an excellent host. He used to like being taken around the East End pubs by the twins. He had business interests in a club in London and we went there on many occasions. I could see that Ronnie loved being in his company. He used to say with unaccustomed humour: 'He is only a gangster in his films. I am one for real!'

I was lucky enough to be asked to go to various London pubs with George Raft and Ronnie in the limousine driven by George Raft's chauffeur. Ronnie wanted to show him off. At times I felt like a film actor just walking around with him. These good times soon came to an end, though. He had to go to France, and we thought we would continue to see him when he came back. But unfortunately he was not allowed back into the country because the police believed he was involved with the Mafia. We heard much later that George had died in France. We were very sorry.

Once we were told that we would be going to a mansion house in Saffron Walden, in Essex, one weekend. It was a big place in the country surrounded by acres of woodland and Ronnie had some business to do there. I drove Ron and Ian and the others went in their own cars.

As we drove into the country Ronnie said: 'One day, I will have my own mansion down here and I will only have a few of the faithfuls with me.'

We made no comment – none was needed.

When we arrived, Jeff, the owner of the mansion, was there to greet us. I recognized him immediately. He always came to London to see the firm in a white Mercedes and he was always treated like royalty. The other cars arrived just after us and we were all invited in for drinks. There was a lot of small talk, and later, as we walked around the grounds, I asked Ian: 'What does he really do for a living?'

'I don't know, he must have his finger in a lot of pies,' he answered.

Only Ronnie ever stayed at the house. The rest of us, including Reggie, were booked into a local hotel. Over the weekend we all noticed that we were being tailed by plain-clothes police, but we didn't know whether they were locals or London officers. It did make us cut the weekend short.

When we arrived back in the East End there was a message for Reggie at the pub where we had all arranged to meet. We didn't know what it was, but the following morning he phoned me at the card club and said: 'You will be taking me up West tonight. Be here at about seven o 'clock.'

'OK,' I said. Then I went back to where Ian sat drinking tea with Billy. 'It looks like I won't see you tonight,' I said. 'I have got to go to the West End. At times I wish I didn't drive, I seem to always be on call.'

I picked Reggie up as planned and I got the same old story that I had heard many times before on other meetings, about how we were going to make plenty of money. This time we were going to meet two Canadians, who were already known to Reggie. They wanted to put a proposition to the firm. When we drove up to the hotel where the meeting was to take place, I did what I had done many times before, driving round, parking the car away from the hotel, and looking around to make sure we weren't being followed. Every time I went on one of these meetings I got the feeling that I was an extra on a film set making a gangster movie.

We made our way into the hotel and up to the cocktail bar. As we entered a man came over. He was wearing a white raincoat and a trilby hat. He shook hands with us. I asked him how long he had been waiting.

'Oh,' he answered, 'about half an hour.'

As we sat down I noticed a man sitting at the next table, close to us. 'Is he with you?' I asked, indicating the man.

'Yes,' said the man in the trilby, 'but he will stay where he is, he knows all about the business on hand.'

Reggie and I looked at each other and I knew that he was thinking the same as me – that this was a setup. I did not like the atmosphere one bit. It seemed strange that the other man did not want to sit at our table. I ordered drinks and the Canadian spoke about forged stamps and plates. After a while he took an envelope out of his raincoat pocket. 'This is what we have been talking about,' he said.

In the envelope were some samples of British saving stamps. He tried very hard to get one of us to handle them, but we wouldn't, just in case it was a frame.

He then said: 'They are very good forgeries. You can have a quarter of a million pounds' worth for as little as £25,000.'

'Why so cheap?' Reggie asked.

'We have so many of them, we want to move them quickly,' he answered.

Reggie then called the waiter over for more drinks and started the same routine as his brother had when I was with him discussing the Tangiers affair, staring round the bar suspiciously. It was at this point that we suspected that the Canadian had more than one other person with him. We felt that other eyes were on us. I could not make up my mind as to whether they were working for the police, or were Canadian villains. We carried on talking as if we were really interested in what they proposed, but Reggie then asked if he could make another meet, because he had to report back to the rest of the firm.

'It has got to be soon,' the Canadian said. 'We will only be here for a few more days.'

He asked Reggie for a phone number where he could get in touch with him.

'That's all right,' Reggie replied, 'we will be back in two days with our answer.'

The Canadian accepted that and we shook hands with him, but the other guy just looked up and nodded, and as we left the cocktail lounge I still had the feeling that we were being observed.

We made our way back to the car and as we drove back to the East End I said to Reggie: 'What are you going to do about this meeting?'

He replied, 'We'll see what Ronnie says.'

We went to the pub where Ronnie was drinking and told him about the meeting with the Canadian, but with all the mistrust that was being felt at this time, we were told to 'leave it out'. The Canadian proposition was just another big waste of time.

Now and then, stories filtered to us on the grapevine

that some Greek villains were moving into the territory that was our domain.

The firm stayed very much on its own territory – the East End and part of the West End – and expected other gangs to do the same. We knew, of course, that other gangs existed – there were, for example, others in East London as well as several Chinese and some South London gangs (of which the Richardsons were the best known). But we had no contact with them, if we could help it.

One night, soon after the Canadian episode, two men with swarthy complexions appeared in one of the pubs that the firm called their own. They walked over to the bar and asked for a drink. One member of the firm must have recognized them from somewhere because he went over to Ronnie and told him they were Greeks from the North London area.

Ronnie got it into his head that they were spying on the firm because suddenly, without any warning, he went straight over to them and started punching them. As usual, some of the firm joined in, and in no time they were a bloody mess. The poor bastards, they were so badly beaten up they had to be taken to the London Hospital.

A few weeks later, another Greek came to the pub

to meet the firm – but this one made an appointment first. He wanted to make a proposition.

'If I can say that I am working with the firm, I can command a fair amount of money from the Greek gaming clubs who know your reputation. The firm would get a good percentage out of it.' He looked round at us hopefully.

Ronnie took an immense liking to this man. He was tall, handsome, in his early thirties and very well dressed. We met him in our pub a few times, then Ian and I went to North London with him to visit some of the Greek-run clubs that he had spoken of. We got on very friendly terms with him, and were allowed into these clubs which normally only let in Greeks.

A few weeks later, Ian and I got a phone call at the card club where we still spent our days. Ronnie wanted to see us right away. We drove over to the house in Vallance Road and he greeted us with: 'The big Greek has died.' We were shocked. We found out that he had suddenly had a heart attack.

'I want you to go round and tell the firm that they have got to go to the funeral,' he said. 'I don't want his crowd to find out he didn't work for us.'

The funeral was like one you would see in a Mafia film. We were all dressed in dark suits. I can remember all the Greek club-owners and friends of his on one side, and the East End gangsters like us on the other. But it didn't do the firm any good after that to try to muscle in on their territory. The Greek club-owners doubled up their minders in all their gaming clubs, making sure that nobody from the East End moved in, and Ronnie told us to keep out of the clubs in the Greek area. 'We don't need any trouble from that direction,' were the words he used. We had met some nice Greek guys, but after that warning from Ronnie, we dropped them all.

The firm weren't so interested when it came to drug dealing. Rumour went round the firm that there was a factory in the country just outside London that was producing purple hearts. They were very powerful pills and in great demand in the West End of London. Some of us were told that if we wanted to get involved with this, we could make a fortune on the black market.

At one of the meetings that we had in the pub, we were asked what our thoughts were on the subject of selling these drugs to the peddlers in the West End. One or two of the firm were sceptical, they started talking among themselves. This was something new to them. We had all been so used in the past to getting our money from the gaming clubs. Now it seemed the twins wanted us to get involved in something very dangerous.

We had to be very careful when we criticized the twins because we didn't know whether we could trust each other. From experience, we all knew that things had a habit of getting back to them. If they discovered that anybody was talking out of turn there was trouble. I, for one, was not in favour of dealing with drugs.

Ian said: 'What about Jack the Hat? He knows everybody that handles dope in the West End. Why doesn't Reggie get him to show a few samples and take orders?'

'You had better put it to Ronnie,' someone said. 'We all know that Jack the Hat has already double-crossed the firm with that vanload of gear.'

'Maybe you're right,' said Ian. 'I don't think it would be such a good idea after all even to mention it to him.'

Unknown to us, the pills were eventually handed over to a man not connected with the firm. I only found this out some days later, when I was sitting in the lounge of the house in Vallance Road waiting for Ronnie to get dressed to go out. There was a knock at the door and I went to answer it. A man stood there who was a stranger to me. He asked if Ronnie was at home. Just as I was going to call him, he came down the stairs – he looked furious. 'What the fuck are you doing here?' he shouted. 'You had better come in.'

The man followed him into a different room. I shut the street door and went back into the lounge. I heard Ronnie screaming at him. He had brought a small parcel with him and Ronnie called me into the room where they were arguing.

'Get this bastard out of here quick,' he yelled, 'and make sure he puts that parcel down some bloody drain.'

The man started to sweat and shake. He said: 'But Ron, they are duds. I have had experts testing them – look for yourself.'

He opened a bag. It contained hundreds of round purple objects that looked like pills.

'I know nothing about them!' screamed Ronnie.

I gave the man the nod to move out, knowing the kind of mood Ronnie was in. I went outside with him and said: 'Where are you going to dump them?'

He said: 'I will get them off my plate quickly.'

I beckoned him to come round the corner with me where there was a drain. We opened it and I said: 'Put them down there, that way we'll know they are not on the streets.'

He dropped them down the drain and I felt relieved now they were destroyed. 'I think you had better keep out of sight until this thing has blown over. You've put Ronnie in a right bad mood,' I told him.

'OK and thanks,' he said.

I went back into the house where Ronnie was still getting ready. He turned to me and asked, 'Do you really think they were duds?'

I looked at him and replied: 'I know nothing about dope and I don't want to. If the law had followed that geezer here we would have been in a lot of trouble.'

Ronnie nodded and asked, 'Did you see him get rid of them?'

'Yes,' I replied. 'We put them down the drain!'

There was no more talk about purple hearts.

CHAPTER 7

JACK THE HAT'S NEW TRICK

We were changing our meeting-places so often now, it was decided that the firm should have a pub of its own. The one chosen was a very small one off the Bethnal Green Road in Cheshire Street, called The Carpenter's Arms. Situated in a narrow street, surrounded by very old houses and shops, it was very much like all the others: very dark inside, but with only one bar. The twins arranged for a very good friend of their father's to look after it. He was a man who had never been in any trouble, and he looked after the bar very well.

One evening I went round to see a man called Bill who, although he was a member of the firm, was only a very small cog. I told him that the firm was opening a bar of its own. I knew that he was not a well man and could not get a regular job.

'Why don't you go round and try to get the barman's job?' I asked him. 'At least you will get a few quid each week.'

He did as I suggested, and asked for the job. They felt sorry for him and he got it.

One night in the pub, the firm were discussing the various clubs that they were taking money from. They were constantly on the lookout for more, it didn't matter whether they had any connection with the firm or not. There was one that we had heard of which had just opened in Stoke Newington and a friend of the owner was drinking in our company – he had been on the firm before my time, way back in 1962. He was talking about this club and saying how well it was doing. Reggie seemed impressed. If it was making money, it might be prepared to pay for protection.

'Go and have a look at it tomorrow,' he told me, 'and take Ian with you.'

Ian and I looked at each other, but we made no comment because we already knew the club. We had been going there pretty regularly and we were both very good friends of Jim, the owner. A few nights later, Reggie asked us if we had been to the new club and how we had got on.

'All right,' I replied, 'the man is only making a living, it's just a small place and not worth bothering about.'

Unknown to me, they sent a couple of the firm to have a look at the club because they didn't believe what I'd said. They reported back and said: 'It's a good club. The firm should get a few quid out of it every week.'

Reggie looked at me, his temper rising. 'I thought you said it was no fucking good.'

I told him that the man was a friend of mine and it would not be fair if they tried to blag him. I repeated that he was only making a living. I tried hard to convince him but it was a waste of time. Later on in the pub, while they were still talking about how they could get money from this new club, I thought to myself: 'Christ! Things must be getting bad again.'

Just then, Jim's friend came into the bar and walked over to where we were sitting.

'Did you get a result from the club I was telling you about?' he asked.

This started Reggie off again. 'You know him, go to the club and tell your friend we need £1,000. You can tell him that we will look after his place for him.'

This was something that the man did not expect. He didn't mind getting Jim involved with the firm, but he didn't want any part of it himself. He had the look of a man who wished he had never opened his mouth. 'Can't you send someone else?' he asked. 'He will know that I have been talking to you about his club if I go and tell him that he has got to give me £1,000 for the firm.'

The twins started screaming and shouting at him, so I said, 'I will go with him.'

They weren't too happy about that because I knew Jim, but I would have said anything to get away from all that noise. They let me go, and when we got outside I said: 'You had no right to get the firm to try to blag money from Jim. You know as well as I do that he can't afford to pay any money for protection.'

He looked worried and said: 'I didn't expect it to go this far.'

We drove to the club in my car and when we walked in I felt like telling Jim about his so-called friend, who had discussed his business with the firm. But I had second thoughts because it would only have caused more bother for us all. However, he must have been tipped off by somebody because when we sat down he came over and offered us a drink. Then he said: 'I can let them have £200, that is all I've got. If that's all right, you can meet me at the Angel Bar tomorrow lunchtime.'

I said: 'Don't worry about it. I will see them in the morning and tell them that you haven't got that kind of money. I will try hard to talk them out of it.'

He was very grateful for any help, so we had another drink with him and left.

The next morning, when I got to the house I was greeted with: 'Well, did you get the grand?'

'The man hasn't got that kind of money,' I said, choosing my words carefully. 'He has put his last few quid into this little drinking club and besides, a lot of our friends use it, you can ask any of them and they will tell you the same.'

I carried on telling them that he was willing to help out and hand over £200. I wished I had not opened my mouth because Ronnie screamed at me: 'Who the fuck does he think he is, offering that kind of money? I spend that on a night out. Go back and tell him that we want what we asked for within the next three weeks.'

I hated the idea of going back and telling Jim that they wouldn't accept the £200. 'They want the full amount in the next few weeks,' I had to tell him.

'Can we leave it at that and I promise I will try and sort something out?' he said.

On one of the meeting nights, Jim's club was brought up again. 'How's that little club doing? Have you had a result yet?'

'It's all right,' I said, but I knew by the look on Ronnie's face that it wasn't the end of it. Just then the door opened and in walked Jack the Hat. I thought to myself, 'You have got to hand it to him. After double-crossing the firm a few weeks ago, in he walks as bold as brass as though nothing had happened.'

'Hello, chaps,' he said brightly, 'how are you all? I haven't seen you for a few weeks. Just thought I would drop in and let you know that I am still about.'

I have never seen so many surprised faces. He was so doped up he couldn't have cared less. He knew that the firm had been looking for him, but he came straight over to the table where we were sitting, rubbing his hands together. 'Sorry I nicked a bit of that gear,' he said happily, 'but I needed the money. I did it on my own and I will make up for it. If you want me to do anything for you, you know you can count on me.'

He was so good with his words he might have been practising before he came into the bar. If anybody deserved an Oscar for a performance, it was him. I thought he had guts that night and we all included him in the drinks that evening. Bad as he was, I couldn't dislike him.

Reggie was getting quite drunk by now and out of the blue he stood up and, turning to Ronnie, said that he was going to the drinking club in North London. As usual, I had to drink with him there. Ronnie pointed to Jack the Hat and whispered to me: 'Take that drunken bastard with you, I don't want him left here with us.'

Jack jumped at the chance to go with us – he really thought that they had forgiven him for the double-cross earlier. 'Where are we going?' he asked.

'We are going to Jim's drinking club,' I said. 'See you there.'

Reggie and I got into my car and there was no conversation on the short drive over. Jack drove his own car. When we arrived at the club and walked in, Jim came over.

'Hello, Reggie, would you like a drink?' he asked. Reggie looked around and said to me: 'I thought you said this place wasn't taking money.'

'It's not that good,' I answered, 'look around, it's half empty.'

Then Jack walked in. Poor Jim, neither he nor anybody else could have foreseen what was to happen in the next few minutes. The man who had originally told the firm about the club came up. 'Hello, Reg,' he said. 'What are you doing here? Would you like a drink?'

Reggie put his hand on his shoulder and, indicating Jim, said: 'Tell that bastard I want to speak to him.'

Jack the Hat got excited. 'What's the matter, what's the matter? Do you want me to do someone for you?' he shouted.

At that a few people who had been drinking at the bar left their drinks and went out quickly. Jim came over and said apologetically: 'I'm sorry that I couldn't help you with money, but as you can see there's not a lot of business here. This is only a little sideline that I have.'

Suddenly, out of the blue, Jack started hitting and kicking him. Within a few seconds he was a terrible mess. I grabbed hold of Jack and dragged him out of the bar. When I got him outside, I yelled: 'Who the fuck told you to do that?'

'Nobody, I'm with Reg,' he said, trying to shrug me off.

I kept hold of him. 'He doesn't need you to fight for him. He only came here for a drink.'

Just then we heard a shot from inside the club. I ran back and Jim was lying on the floor, bleeding from the beating up he had just got from Jack and from the bullet that had entered his foot.

'If we tell you to pay up, we are not fooling around. This is just a warning,' said Reggie coldly.

Jim was being helped up by his so-called friend.

'You had better get him home,' I said.

As I spoke, Reggie handed the gun to Jack and told him to get rid of it right away. Then he ordered me to take him to one of the hide-outs that were used at various times when violence erupted. It had happened again. Reggie had shot someone when he was drunk and everybody else was involved by having to do all the dirty work – like disposing of the gun, calling the Doc, and taking Reggie to a hide-out. Twenty-four hours later it was all over the East End that someone had been shot. Everybody knew who had done it but the wall of silence went up again as usual. I thought that the police must surely be told by their informers what was going on, yet they were keeping a very low profile.

A few nights later, when we were all in the pub having a drink, in walked Jim's 'friend'.

'How's your mate?' I called out to him.

'He's all right now,' he answered. 'He says that he has had enough and he is closing down the drinking club.'

'It was all your fault what happened to him,' I cut in. His face reddened, but he carried on speaking.

'He doesn't want any more aggro, but he didn't go to the police, the Doc patched him up all right.'

Later that evening Reggie came into the pub and beckoned to me. I went over to him and he put his hand on my shoulder and whispered: 'Who did I give my gun to that night?'

'Christ,' I replied. 'Can't you remember? You gave it to Jack the Hat. You told him to get rid of it.'

Knowing what type of person Jack was, he got into a bit of a flap. 'You had better go over to his house,' he said, 'and ask him if he got rid of it.'

I had a couple of drinks with the boys and left the pub to drive over to Jack's house. When I got there he told me that he had not been out since the shooting. 'What happened the other night?' he asked. 'Why did Reggie shoot that geezer? I had already done what I was told to do and I gave him a good hiding – there was no need for Reggie to shoot him.'

'Nobody asked you to beat him up,' I said. 'It would never have got out of hand – Reggie only wanted to talk to him.'

Jack looked a bit confused. 'He's fucking mad, just like his brother,' he said.

'I wouldn't go around saying things like that if I were you,' I told him.

Jack knew how dangerous they were, but he said: 'I don't care about them, I can look after myself.'

Just then, his girlfriend came into the room with a cup of tea. She was a big girl and cared a lot about Jack. His past was no secret to her, but she stood by him and always said that one day he would change and settle down.

After she left the room, he said: 'What brought you over here anyway?'

'I came to find out what happened to the gun that you were supposed to get rid of – can you remember? Reggie gave it to you at the club.'

'Oh yes,' he said, calmly sipping his tea. 'I smashed it up and put it in the dustcart. Tell him not to worry, it's gone for ever.'

Knowing him as I did, I somehow found it hard to believe that he had really got rid of the gun. He was far too unreliable – although he might have meant to do it at the time.

'I hear they are going to spring Frank Mitchell to do a job for them,' he said suddenly.

'Who's Mitchell?' I asked perplexedly.

'What!' he asked, looking equally puzzled. 'Don't tell me you don't know him? Everybody in London knows Big Frank.'

Jack went to a cabinet in the corner of the room and poured out a couple of drinks. I took one and he carried on talking. 'I've heard that they have been sending some of the firm down to Dartmoor Prison to see him. If they want me to go on a visit I will be glad to. I know a lot of the cons there.' He went on to boast that he had been inside with Mitchell for a time.

I thought, 'This is very interesting, he is telling me something I don't know.' He mentioned the names of one or two villains that he knew in Dartmoor. Because I was silent he looked at me and, realizing that I had not heard about this from the firm, he changed the subject. He went on to tell me that he and his girlfriend would like to settle down and have a family. I knew he was just dreaming – he couldn't go straight if he tried.

'You will have to keep off the dope first,' I told him.

'Yeah! Yeah! Of course I will,' he answered laughingly.

I looked at my watch and jumped to my feet. 'I have to go now, Jack. I will have to report back to them and reassure them that you have got rid of the gun.'

He laughed again, 'Yeah! Yeah! You tell them it is well out of the way.'

I called out goodbye to his girlfriend and let myself out.

When I got back to the pub, I went over and whispered to Reggie: 'It's all right. Jack has got rid of it.'

He looked relieved. 'Are you sure?' he asked.

'Yes, I don't think he would lie to me,' I told him. He seemed to accept this, but it was a known practice among some members of the firm to tell the twins only what they thought would please them, so as to avoid trouble.

CHAPTER 8

'THE MAD AXEMAN' ON THE LOOSE

One evening, a few of the firm were having a drink. Everything was quiet in the East End. There had been no arrests for the shootings and no questions asked, and a few of us, discussing it among ourselves, could not understand it. Could the law not touch the twins? Or, as some of us were thinking, were they playing a waiting game? It was now 1966 and I had been with the firm for two years.

In the passing weeks, members of the firm were sent to various prisons all over the country to see certain friends of the twins and find out if they needed anything. There was one man in particular that they gave a lot of attention to. His name was Frank Mitchell, otherwise known to the Underworld as 'The Mad Axeman'. This was the man Jack the Hat had mentioned to me – Big Frank. Frank Mitchell had the reputation for being a violent man and difficult to control. He had spent half his life in prison for robbery with violence. As he admitted to me later, he had also attempted to murder another prisoner. He was called 'The Mad Axeman' because once, when he had escaped from prison, he picked up an axe from an old couple's yard and had supposedly threatened the couple with it. Now he was in his early thirties and being held in Dartmoor Prison.

It was around this time that Ronnie moved for a brief spell into a flat in Finchley, North London. One evening I was at the club playing cards when I received a phone call from Ronnie, asking me to go to see him at the flat. As usual, I had to leave in the middle of a game – and that always met with great disapproval from the other players. However, I had got to go. It took me about one-and-a-half hours to get there because it was unfamiliar territory to me and I had to make sure I was not being followed. I drove off the main road into a cul-de-sac where the block of flats was.

I knocked at the door and it was opened by a man that I had never seen before. I hesitated, thinking I was at the wrong flat. But he was expecting me because he said: 'Ronnie is waiting for you.'

I followed him into a lounge where Ronnie was sitting. He stood up and said to me: 'This is Teddy. He is a very old friend of mine.'

Teddy was tall, with dark curly hair; he was about thirty years old and very smartly dressed. By the way they laughed and joked, it appeared they had a lot in common. Teddy also liked to be around young men.

'Is your car in good running order?' Ronnie asked me. 'Do you think it would go on a long journey without breaking down?'

I felt a nagging suspicion about this question. 'I wouldn't want to drive it too far, it is only an 1100,' I told him.

'Pat and Teddy are going down to Dartmoor Prison to see an old friend of mine,' he said. 'Would you mind driving them down in your car?'

'It's only a small car,' I said, thinking about the size of Big Pat, 'and I don't think it would take the distance.'

Luckily this was almost the first time he had asked me to do something, so I took advantage of his good mood, which was so rare, and declined to go. He was quite cheerful about my refusal, which surprised me, and I couldn't believe my good fortune. I was in no mood for driving people backwards and forwards to Dartmoor Prison.

Unknown to the firm, though Jack had hinted at it, Teddy (a very old friend of Ronnie's but not a member of the firm) and another man had already been down to Dartmoor to see Frank Mitchell. It was easy to visit him because he was with an outside party, which meant that he was a trusted prisoner – he was out on the moors working instead of being locked up all day in his cell. He could even go to the local pub for a drink as long as he was back at the right time to be counted.

A few days later Fat Wally came to the club to see me one afternoon. He was looking worried. 'Teddy has just been on the phone to me,' he said, 'and he has had a message from Ronnie that I have to give him my car for a few days. Have you got any idea what he wants it for? You know that I can't do without my car – how will I get around?'

I laughed and said: 'Tell him what I told him, that your car is not a very good runner.'

Wally looked doubtful and said: 'You know what he is like, he will do his nut if I tell him that and he finds out I am lying. Can you do me a favour and tell him that for me?'

Wally was understandably scared because the last time they wanted his car he had got involved in

Nobby's shootings. I felt a bit sorry for him but I had to say that there was no way I could get in touch with Ronnie unless he wanted me to. Wally then left and went back to his club. Later, Bill, barman at the pub, came to see me.

'I thought you were working in the pub,' I said, surprised at his visit.

'Ronnie has taken me out of it,' he replied. 'He wants me to go to a house in Barking, in Essex, and stay there with someone called Lennie. He sent a message telling me that a friend of his will be coming to stay for a few days and he wants me to keep him company at this Len's place. It's the same old fucking thing, they have put me on a promise for doing this favour.'

I laughed to myself – I had also heard those promises – but he kept on grumbling. 'You know what their promises are like. I thought I might have carried on working in the pub – at least I was getting my wages. I am fed up with this kind of life – they only want to use people.'

Bill was really getting into the swing of it now. 'It's coming up to Christmas,' he complained, 'and I have a lot of things to do. It's all right for them in their gold watches and new suits, I can't remember the last time I could afford a suit.'

I listened to this, and then I had an idea. 'Why don't you ask them for a new suit?' I said, knowing that they had given Ian money to buy one.

He just looked at me and grinned. I felt sorry for him – he was always being used. He sat at the table with his hand on his forehead. 'I suppose I will have to do it for them,' he sighed. Then his face brightened as if he had had an idea: 'Why don't you tell them that you will take my place?'

I nearly choked on my cup of tea. 'How the hell can I go and say that when I am not supposed to know what they want you to do? You shouldn't even have told me about it. You should know better than to tell anybody their plans. Anyway, I will be going to Scotland in a few days' time for Christmas and New Year.'

Bill started again: 'This is definitely the last favour I am doing for them. I don't care – I am getting out before things get any worse.'

'Do you really think you will be able to walk away from all this and live to tell the tale?' I asked, surprised at the way he was talking, but Bill knew that what he said to me wouldn't be repeated.

On one of his visits Frank Mitchell told Teddy that he didn't have a release date. Because of this he was getting very depressed. Teddy told the twins about this and they sent a message back to Frank saying that they would arrange for his escape so that he could write to the papers and state his case. Then, with the newspapers' help, when he got a release date he would go back to prison and serve his sentence.

This was quite a challenge to the twins and, if successful, would prove that they could do anything and get away with it. Presumably everything went according to plan because I was summoned to the flat in Finchley by Ronnie. When I got there, he said: 'I want you to go over to a place in Barking to stay with a friend of mine. Bill is there now and I want you to give him a break so that his wife doesn't get worried.'

'I can't,' I answered. 'I told you a few weeks ago that I was going up to see my family in Scotland for Christmas and the New Year.'

'You will just have to put it off,' he replied.

He told me that he had arranged for Frank Mitchell's escape. 'Teddy will go to Barking with you,' he said. 'He is going to write some letters for Frank to send to the newspapers. He will write and say Frank wants them to know that he is one of the few prisoners who have not got a release date. And he thinks that if he brings it to the notice of the authorities via the newspapers, they may do something about it.'

'It must be terrible,' I said, 'for a man to be locked up without knowing when he will be freed.'

Ronnie nodded. 'He will go back inside after the letters have been printed.' Then he changed the subject. 'I don't want you to take your car to Barking, instead I want you to meet Teddy at Whitechapel station at six o'clock tonight and he will take you over there. Don't tell anybody else where you are going.'

I nodded and left. On my way back to the East End I noticed that the police were out in full force. I presumed that they had been told about Mitchell's escape and would be visiting their informants to see if any of them knew where he was holed up. I knew that their efforts would be fruitless. Hardly anybody knew about Mitchell's escape – and if they did they wouldn't dare inform on the firm.

I met Teddy as arranged and it was the usual cloak-and-dagger stuff, making sure we were not being followed. The flat in Barking was on the ground floor and looked very nice from the outside. When we got to the front door, Teddy gave a special pre-arranged knock. The door was opened immediately by a grey-haired thin man of about fifty-five who was wearing glasses. Teddy had already met him.

'Hello, Len! Everything all right?' He handed him an envelope. 'Ronnie sent this over to you to get some food with. He said that he would pay you off later.'

Up until now, we had been standing in the small hallway, but as we followed Lennie into the living room I thought, 'I have heard that one before from a few other people.'

As Lennie and I were introduced, I glanced round and saw Bill sitting at the dining-room table. He looked very surprised to see me there as I had told him I was going up to Scotland. He nodded to Teddy and told him that Frank was in the bedroom. Teddy went to the bedroom door and tapped on it. He called out: 'It's only me, Frank.'

After a couple of seconds, Frank came out. I had never seen him before and was surprised to see such a giant of a man, dressed only in a pair of jeans, who could easily have been taken for Charles Atlas.

Teddy introduced me to Frank and told him: 'He will be staying here to keep you company for a few days. Bill can't stay here all the time – he has a wife and children to look after.'

When we shook hands, it was as if mine was held in a vice, he was so strong. He towered over me. He must have been at least six-feet three-inches tall and extremely broad, with what I considered were very good looks.

'Have you got any writing paper and envelopes, Len?' Teddy asked. 'We want to start on Frank's letters as soon as possible.'

Lennie had to think for a moment, then he went into the kitchen and we heard him searching through the drawers. He came back into the living room waving the paper and envelopes. 'That's all I've got,' he said, handing them to Teddy. 'Will that be enough?'

Teddy took them and said: 'That's fine. Will you make a pot of tea before we get started?'

Bill stood up. 'You don't really need me here any more, I think I will have it away,' he said, as Frank and Teddy sat at the table and prepared to write the letters to the papers.

As Bill walked into the bedroom to pick up his few things, I followed him. He was moaning like hell: 'I have been here all fucking night – my wife doesn't even know where I am – she must be getting frantic. They wouldn't even let me phone her.' He was rushing around the room wiping everything clean with his handkerchief. I looked at him in amazement, wondering what had gotten into him.

'What the hell are you doing now?' I asked. He carried on with his antics of cleaning the room and answered: 'If Frank gets nicked in this flat, I don't want my fingerprints all over the place.'

'Well,' I said, 'I was told by Teddy that he will give himself up as soon as he gets his release date. That is the only reason they have arranged all this.'

'Huh!' said Bill in a dry voice. 'Just you wait until you have been with him for twenty-four hours, then you will see for yourself whether he has got any intention of giving himself up.'

His words worried me. I hoped it wasn't going to be as difficult as Bill had just indicated getting Frank back to Dartmoor.

Before he left, Bill went into the living room to see Frank. 'Bye for now, and good luck to you,' he said.

Frank looked up from the table and said to Bill: 'Will I see you again? Are you coming back?'

Bill smiled at him, 'You might – but good luck anyway.'

He said goodbye to us and Len went to the door first to check there was nobody around outside on the stairs. He turned back to Bill and called: 'It's all clear – you can go.'

Teddy had started writing samples of letters for Frank to copy. Frank, being rather illiterate, wrote about twenty copies which were not usable and were subsequently thrown away. Eventually, two hours later and after going through several writing pads – which Lennie was sent out to purchase – he finally got a couple completed, to Teddy's great relief: 'All I am asking for,' he wrote, 'is a date of release. From a young age I have not been free. I am not a murderer, nor a danger to the general public.'

'Do you think this will do?' asked Frank anxiously. 'I don't mind going back to prison, if only they would give me a release date.'

I genuinely think that he would not have minded going back, even if he did have to spend another twenty years behind bars, provided that the authorities could give him some hope that he would eventually be released. Teddy got up from the table and stretched. 'I have got to go now,' he said, yawning. 'I think I have been here long enough. After Ronnie has read the letter, I will take them somewhere else, out of this manor, and post them to the *Mirror* and *The Times*.'

Lennie then did the same for Teddy as he had done for Bill. He went outside and made sure the coast was clear – after all, we were harbouring an escaped prisoner from a top-security prison!

The street door was opened by Lennie, so Teddy whispered to Frank: 'I will be seeing you Frank. Good luck.'

The door closed and Teddy was gone, leaving just Lennie and I to look after Frank. Lennie went out into the kitchen to cook us a meal and Frank said excitedly: 'Do you think they will print the letters in the newspapers?'

'Of course they will,' I told him encouragingly. 'I wouldn't be surprised if you don't see your face on TV. After all, it is not often that someone escapes from Dartmoor and gets clean away.'

He started to tell me how easy everything had been with the escape. 'I always knew in advance what days I would be working on the moors. Some of the prison officers let me wander off to feed the wild horses. As long as I was back for counting they didn't bother me. The escape was planned weeks ago.'

He was so grateful to the twins for arranging his escape from prison that he kept telling me that Ronnie was his best pal.

Just then Lennie interrupted as he came into the room with our meals. Frank's meal, in particular, must have contained at least one pound of steak. I looked at his plate stacked high with food and I thought: 'Christ, where does he put it?' The evening passed with us watching Frank doing his exercises. He was a fanatic about building up his body and keeping fit.

CHAPTER 9

THE MITCHELL EPISODE

The following morning, Bill came into the flat while Frank was bathing and Lennie was out shopping. He came into the living room and whispered: 'How did you get on last night with Frank?'

'All right,' I whispered back, 'but he keeps telling me that he wants a girl.'

'What girl is going to come here?' asked Bill, looking annoyed. 'It's all over the papers who he is. It's been three days since he was brought here and I am not going to be doing this too long. What chance would he have if the police were tipped off that he was here? No chance, and we would be left holding the bag. We would get no fucking help from anybody.'

I told him to keep his voice down but he carried on: 'It's all right for them [meaning the twins], they have the money to buy their way out of this. I have a family to think of. My wife is scared to be on her own at night. I want to see Ronnie – do you know where he is?'

'Yes, I do,' I replied, 'but do you really think they will let you out now?'

As we were speaking, Frank came out of the bathroom. He was wearing a new shirt that Len had bought him earlier.

'Hello, Frank,' Bill said, smiling at him. 'You look good.'

'I will be seeing Ron later,' I said to Bill. 'I am going to ask him if he will get someone else to take my place here because, as you know, I am supposed to be going to Scotland for Christmas and the New Year. I might as well leave now.'

They said 'Cheerio', and I left them and went over to Finchley. Ronnie answered the door and let me in. He was alone, sitting drinking and listening to records. As I followed him into the lounge, he said over his shoulder: 'You have just missed Teddy. He has gone back over to Barking to help Frank write to a few more newspapers. How is he getting on there? Is he causing any bother?'

He sounded genuinely interested.

'At the moment he's all right,' I said, 'but he wants

a bird, and if you don't get him one while he's in this frame of mind, he will go out and get one himself, and we won't be able to stop him.'

Ronnie's whole attitude changed and he jumped up, shouting, 'That ungrateful bastard! Who does he think he is? He will drop us all in it if he starts that bloody caper – I have my own troubles.'

He sat down again and lit a cigarette and told me to pour the drinks that were on the coffee table in front of him. He stared over his glasses broodingly, thinking. It looked as if he was in another world – there was nothing said for about five minutes, but it seemed like an hour. Then he spoke.

'Go back and tell him not to worry, we will arrange for a girl. Tell him to be patient and everything will work out all right for him.'

His attitude had completely changed again. 'Who's looking after him at this moment?' he asked.

'Bill's there just now, but he is not happy with the situation,' I replied. 'I am not due back there until tomorrow. Is there any chance of you getting someone else to take my place? It's a bit nerve-racking being with him. All he does is exercise, and he keeps diving into the bathroom to clean his teeth – he's going to run out of toothbrushes and paste at this rate – I have never known such a clean-teeth fanatic.'

Ronnie gave one of his strange laughs. 'I don't want too many of the firm to know that we have had anything to do with Mitchell's escape, you know what they are for talking in the pubs.' His voice got serious. 'I've heard a whisper that the law has been making enquiries around the East End about the escape and I don't think it is just local coppers. There's one called "Nipper Read" who has been after me for years.'

Ronnie carried on talking. 'Tell Bill it won't be too long before we move Frank to the country, where he will stay on a farm. It's not easy for me being cooped up here, but I am busy trying to make all the arrangements. You will still be able to go to Scotland for your New Year.'

Reggie came in and Ronnie told him: 'He's going back over to the flat in Barking. I have given him a few messages for Mitchell.'

I sat down again, I wanted to hear what Reggie was going to say to Ronnie, but he dismissed me. 'You can go now, we will be in touch.'

When I got back to Barking I was let in by Len, who looked surprised to see me. 'What are you doing here?' he asked. 'You are not supposed to come back here until tomorrow.'

I didn't answer him, I just walked into the living room. Teddy was already there, sitting at the table with Frank writing more letters. I turned to Bill, who was sitting reading a paper. I told him that he could go home to his wife if he liked, now that I was there – I would stay in his place.

'Did you ask them about a bird?' asked Frank.

'Yes, they are going to arrange it as soon as they can,' I replied, hoping it would be soon.

By this time, Teddy had finished writing the letters. He and Bill left together, leaving Lennie and me with Frank – who was getting very excited at the prospect of a girl coming to stay with him. He kept on walking up and down between the living room and the street door doing breathing exercises and flexing his muscles. One would have thought he was going on his first date.

It was now about 10.30 in the evening. 'Where is she?' he asked, getting very impatient. 'Are you sure they are sending a bird out? I haven't had a bird for years and I have a lot of time to make up for.'

I couldn't help laughing – he was just like a kid in his excitement.

At about twelve o'clock the phone rang twice, then stopped. This was a pre-arranged signal with Len for answering the phone. We waited for a few seconds, then the phone rang again, as expected. Len picked it up, listened for a moment, then put it down. He spoke to Frank in an excited voice: 'The girl will be coming over here at about two in the morning.'

Frank got up off his chair and said: 'I am going to have a bath and clean my teeth.'

I felt sorry for Lennie. He was rather a nervous person who had his own little business – a second-hand bookstall in the East End. He had never been involved with the firm before though he was a friend of Reggie's. This was his flat and he didn't even have a bed to sleep in. Frank had his bedroom and Bill and I took turns to use the small one – which left Lennie with the settee. He had to be accessible to answer the street door.

Frank came out of the bathroom, and Lennie poured us out a drink to celebrate. To pass the time while we were waiting, we each tried to describe what she would look like. It was funny at the time, because Frank said: 'I hope she will be blonde and tall like me. I have never had sex with a blonde. The last time I had sex with a bird was about a year ago when I was working on an outside party and I met a bird from the local pub. She made arrangements to see me and we had sex on the moors. The prison

Above: Reggie and Ronnie in their teens pictured with their mum, Violet.

Below: Reggie (*right*) could have had a great future in boxing. If he had stuck with it he might have enjoyed a very different kind of celebrity.

Above: The Blind Beggar pub on Whitechapel Road, east London (*left*), where Ronnie killed George Cornell (*right*), a member of the Richardson Gang.

©Getty Images

Below: A photograph of the interior of the Blind Beggar, taken shortly after the shooting.

©PA Photos

Above: The Kray twins outside their house on Vallance Road. Ronnie is shaking hands with their grandfather, Jimmy, while Reggie puts his arm round their adored mother, Violet. ©*Getty*

Below: Reggie and Frances Shea's wedding in 1965. Ronnie is kissing the bride as Charlie (*left*) looks on. She committed suicide two years later.

©*Rex Features*

'The Mad Axeman', Frank Mitchell, leaves a police station in Hampshire, re-arrested after his escape from Broadmoor 36 hours earlier. Despite his name, I found him to be a gentle giant. He spent most of his short life in various prisons.

©Getty Images

The house on Evering Road in Stoke Newington, London, where Jack McVitie, better known as 'Jack the Hat' (*inset*), met his death.

©*PA Photos / Getty Images*

Above: The twins at the El Morocco nightclub with actor George Sewell (who was later in *Get Carter*) and actress Barbara Windsor.

Below: Ronnie and Reggie out on the town with Judy Garland, one of their favorite celebrities, and her husband Mark Herron.   ©*Getty Images*

Reggie lights a cigarette for Ronnie as the two relax over a cup of tea in
the house on Vallance Road.

Above: (*From left to right*) Christopher Lambrianou, John Barrie, Charlie Kray, Cornelius Whitehead and Reginald Kray, on their way to the Old Bailey in 1969.

Below: The twins' last public appearance. Under tight security, Ronnie (*left*) and Reggie (*right*) were allowed to attend their mother's funeral in Chingford, Essex, in 1982. Both were handcuffed to detectives and led away immediately after the service.

©*Rex Feature*

officers were only a mile away – if only they had known they would all have wanted a bit!'

He told us that if he was nice to the prison officers, and kept out of trouble, then he could work on the moors any time he wished. It seemed strange that a man doing a life sentence at Dartmoor Prison could roam about the moors freely. He had, after all, a record of robbery with violence.

It must have been about 2.30 in the morning when we heard somebody coming. Len was at the door very quickly because he didn't want them to knock in case they disturbed the other tenants living in the block. As the girl walked into the room with one of the firm, I looked at Frank's face. He had the look of a man who couldn't believe his luck. She was just the way he had described the girl he wanted: big, blonde and very attractive. She knew right away which one of us was Frank Mitchell, probably from his picture, which had been on television when he escaped.

'Hello, Frank!' she greeted him with a smile. 'My name is Lisa. I have heard a lot about you.'

At that moment Frank fell in love.

The member of the firm who had brought her over to the flat now made his way to the door: 'I will leave you now, Frank,' he said. 'Have a good time and be gentle with her, she is a very good friend of the firm.' He smiled as he said this, and Frank smiled in reply. He certainly wasn't going to need any encouragement and Lisa knew what she was there for.

We all sat down and Len poured us a drink, but we wanted to go to bed. Earlier in the day Frank had asked Len to purchase a box of chocolates for him to give the girl when she arrived. Frank told Lisa that he had a present for her. 'Will you come and get it?' he asked her.

'Yes, all right,' she answered.

He took her hand and led her into the bedroom. At the door he stopped and, turning back to us, said: 'Goodnight, we will see you in the morning.'

I had to laugh – it was already morning. The bedroom door closed behind them, and Len and I looked at each other and smiled. I spent a very restless night, it was very hard for me to get to sleep. I must have heard Frank get up several times during the night to clean his teeth. I was relieved when morning came and I got up at about 10.30. Len was already in the kitchen cooking our breakfast. By the amount of food he had prepared, one would have thought he was cooking for an army. He took breakfast into the bedroom for

Frank and Lisa, and it was about one o 'clock when they came out of the room.

'Christ!' she exclaimed, 'He is like a stallion – he hasn't stopped all night.'

She was wearing a black negligée, and I commented, 'You look very nice this morning.'

'Thanks,' she replied, 'but I wouldn't want too many nights like that.'

We all laughed and Frank said to me, 'When you see Ronnie, tell him that I need some money. I want to buy Lisa a Christmas present, she has been so good to me.'

I nodded understandingly. 'OK, Frank,' I said, 'I will give him your message.'

He then decided to take a bath and disappeared into the bathroom leaving Lisa and I alone.

'What do you think of him?' I asked her.

She looked at me thoughtfully and said: 'He is so gentle with me, I have never known anybody to be like that with me before. I would like to know how long I will have to be here with him. When Reggie came to the club where I work, he told me that I would only be here for a couple of nights.'

I also looked thoughtful for a moment, then I said slowly, 'I hope so, Lisa, I have been here too long already.'

Just then, Frank came out of the bathroom wearing jeans and a string vest. He started to do press-ups and exercises, flexing his muscles. After we all had lunch, they went back into the bedroom and stayed there till early evening, when Teddy came back to the flat to write the last letter to the newspapers. This time even Lisa joined in, trying to tell them what to write. When it was finished, Teddy stood up.

'I won't be coming back here again,' he said, 'I have done what I was asked to do by the twins.'

Frank nodded and shook his hand. 'Will I be seeing you again?' he asked.

Teddy also nodded and said, 'Yes, of course you will.'

I couldn't help but sense something in his voice that didn't sound right.

When Teddy left the flat, Frank said to Lisa: 'That was the man who helped me to escape from Dartmoor Prison. It was so easy,' he continued. 'I was in London before anybody missed me. Ronnie told me that he is taking me to stay in the country – will you come with me, Lisa?'

At that question, Lisa looked surprised and said: 'I thought you were going to give yourself up after you got your letters printed in the papers?'

Frank's voice suddenly rose. 'I am not going back to Dartmoor – the police will have to shoot me before I ever give myself up. I have been inside too long. I want to see my family – I haven't seen them for years.'

He was starting to get rather agitated. To calm him down, Lisa suggested that they go into the bedroom. Later, when they joined us again in the living room, Frank told Lennie that she was the best thing to happen to him for years. It seemed to me that, although Lisa was not in love with him, she obviously did sincerely care for him.

I went into the kitchen with Lennie. He liked to keep watch on the street by looking out of the kitchen window, which faced that way. He turned as I entered and I could see he had something on his mind.

'They promised me that I would be paid for letting them use my flat and all I have been given is a few quid to buy food for them in the other room.' He glanced at the door to make sure the others couldn't hear him. 'It can't go on much longer. I am bound to be missed at my bookstall. I only agreed to do this for a couple of days because Charlie asked me. I have been there for years and my regulars will miss me. I reckon it's been too long already and it's making me very nervous. I am missing all the Christmas trade and no matter what I get from them now, I will still be out of pocket.'

He broke off because Frank came into the kitchen while we were speaking – but he must have caught the tail end of the conversation.

'What did they say they would give you for looking after me?' he asked Lennie.

Lennie said, 'I was promised £500 for letting you stay here for three days.'

Frank didn't answer. He went into the bedroom, and when he came out he handed Len some money. 'Here, take that,' he told Lennie, 'and we will have a good Christmas.'

This money had been given to Frank by one of the firm, from the twins, on the night of his escape.

'No, I can't take your money,' Lennie said, trying to give the money back to Frank. 'Don't worry,' he continued, 'I will get what they have promised me.'

At that moment there was a knock at the street door. We weren't expecting anybody and we all looked at each other. Frank ran into the living room and grabbed hold of Lisa. He hurried her into the bedroom. Lennie went to open the door. Bill was standing there and Lennie looked very surprised to see him. 'What are you doing here?' he asked. 'You are not supposed to be here until tomorrow.'

Bill walked into the living room and said: 'I have come over to make sure that I have not left anything in the flat that will connect me with harbouring Frank.'

Lisa heard Bill's voice and came into the living room where we were talking. Bill was saying, 'I won't be coming back any more. They got word to me that Frank will be OK with Lisa here.'

Lisa came over to me and whispered: 'I can't stay here forever.'

I said to Lisa: 'Call Frank in, but don't tell him what you just told me.'

I suggested that we all played a game of cards to pass the time away. Bill stayed for a while, but after a couple of hands Frank started getting moody. We didn't know what to do to keep him amused.

He suddenly got up from the table and said: 'Do you want to see how strong I am?'

Just to please him we all said 'Yes'. He flexed his muscles and told Bill and I to stand one on either side of him. Then he held our belts and lifted us both up in the air, one in each hand, with all the ease in the world. He was happy again now that he had shown us how strong he was.

At about 11.30 Bill got up. 'I will have to go now,' he said, 'I have a bus to catch. I won't be seeing you here again, Frank, I have heard that you will be going to the country with Ronnie.' He put out his hand to shake hands with Frank, 'Goodbye and good luck.'

Frank shook hands and said warmly: 'Thanks for everything.'

After Bill left the flat, Lisa said, 'I think I will have a bath. Is there any hot water, Lennie?'

'Yes, Lisa, plenty,' he answered.

While Lisa was in the bathroom, Frank started to get frustrated. 'Ronnie promised me he would come and see me,' he complained. 'I have been here for nine days now and not one of the twins has been near me. I had more fucking freedom in Dartmoor. At least I wasn't cooped up – I could get out and see a bit of sunshine.' He was really getting wound up now. 'How long do they think they can keep me here? I want to see Ronnie. He's fucking letting me down – if he doesn't get here fast I will be looking for him. He was supposed to have me out of London days ago.'

During these ravings I just sat, as I couldn't get a word in. I remember thinking about all the promises that the twins had made to other members of the firm, including myself, and had then forgotten to carry them out. I also got a strong feeling that Frank was getting too hot to handle. He was extremely moody and, knowing that he was called the Mad Axeman, I wondered whether it had been such a good idea getting him out of prison and taking it for granted that he would go back peacefully.

The flat was full of tension. Lennie was not feeling too good – he was letting it show that he was having regrets. After all, it was almost Christmas and he had lost out on trade. I now felt that he would not get the £500 that was promised to him, and I reckoned that he knew it too. As far as he was concerned, it had all been for nothing. I tried to boost his morale. 'Don't worry,' I said. 'They won't let you do this favour for nothing.'

He looked at me and knew I was lying.

Just then, Lisa came out of the bathroom. She was a happy type of girl, but the strain of the past days was beginning to show on her face – even make-up couldn't hide that. She tried to look cheerful. 'Let's all have a Christmas dinner tomorrow! I will cook it and we will see if we can get Bill to come over too.'

I shook my head. 'Bill can't come over, he has a wife and kids and I don't think I will be here – I am hoping to go up North tomorrow for the New Year.' I turned to Frank, who had been sitting silent. 'If you are here over the holiday, Ronnie will send someone else to keep you company.'

Frank jumped angrily to his feet and shouted: 'I don't need anybody to look after me, I can take care of myself. Fuck the lot of you!'

Lisa started to cry, 'Oh Frank, don't carry on like that, you will spoil Christmas.'

Just then, the phone rang twice and stopped. Then it rang again. We all knew it was one of the firm and Lennie answered it. He listened to the voice on the other end and when he put down the receiver he said to Frank, 'Someone is coming to see you.'

Frank jumped up and said excitedly: 'Who is it? Is it Ronnie?' Before Lennie had a chance to reply, he continued: 'I knew he wouldn't let me down. We have been good friends for years and he has always been good to me.'

I sat watching all this and thought how changeable Frank was, one minute he didn't want Ronnie, now he had him back on a pedestal, raving about what a good pal he was. I am sure that if Ronnie had chosen to come over to see Frank and had ordered him to do some diabolical deed for him, he would have jumped at the chance.

CHAPTER 10

THE FINAL
ESCAPE

It wasn't long before we heard the special knock on the street door. Lennie answered, and in walked Reggie with another member of the firm. I could see that they were both uneasy. It was the first time that either of the twins had been over to the flat to see Frank since his escape.

'Hello, Frank,' Reggie said, as he entered the living room.

Frank looked pleased to see him and said: 'Thanks for coming to see me, is Ronnie coming over soon?'

Reggie didn't look Frank straight in the eye and he kept his head down as he answered. 'Ronnie is coming over to pick you up tomorrow, and you and him will be spending the New Year in the country.'

I sensed something wrong as I knew that it would

be impossible for Ronnie to be here the next evening because he was in hiding at the flat in Finchley. But Reggie had Lisa and Len convinced that Frank was going with Ronnie to stay on the farm, and it sounded good to them. I wasn't so sure, but I kept my thoughts to myself.

'I want to take Lisa with me,' Frank said. 'She has been so good the last few days and I don't want to leave without her.'

During the time that I had known Reggie, I had never known him to let anybody tell him what to do. In different circumstances, he would probably have shouted Frank down, but not this time. He kept his cool and said: 'If Lisa wants to go, then we will arrange for her to come down later.'

Frank interrupted. 'I don't want her to come down later; I want her to come down with me when Ronnie picks me up!'

Lisa just sat, staring at Frank and agreeing with everything he said. Something was wrong here, I knew, but I couldn't put my finger on it. I kept looking at Reggie but his face was expressionless and he was giving nothing away.

'If he is getting picked up tomorrow by Ronnie,' I said, 'I think I will try and catch my train to Scotland. They don't need me here.'

Reggie looked at me coldly and replied: 'Ronnie said that he wants you to stay here until he picks up Frank. We have already told Bill that there is no need for him to come back to the flat.'

Now that all the arrangements had been made, and Frank was convinced that he was going with Ronnie to the country, the atmosphere eased considerably, and Frank started to show Reggie how strong he was. But Reggie wasn't impressed and his impatience showed. All he wanted now was to get out of the flat. He humoured Frank for a few minutes then got up to leave. As he did so, he said: 'I will be down to see you and Ronnie on the farm next week – who knows, we might even get you out of the country.'

Reggie told the man who had come with him to go outside and check that there was nobody about in the street. Then he said goodbye and they both left.

I don't think any of us slept much that night. The four of us had a bit of a party – we felt so pleased for Frank. His excitement seemed to rub off onto all of us. It must have been about four in the morning when Lisa said to Frank: 'I think we had better go to bed now. You have quite a long journey ahead of you tomorrow evening.'

I stood up and said to Frank: 'I will probably be

gone in the morning before you get up. There is no need for me to stay here any longer.'

I tried to say goodbye to him, but he kept on asking me to stay until Ronnie came over to pick him up. 'If you stay,' he said pleadingly, 'you might be able to talk him into letting Lisa come with me.'

I looked at him doubtfully and said: 'I don't think my being here will make any difference to Ronnie – no one can tell him what to do – and I don't think I would even try.'

Lisa had been listening to this conversation quietly, then she turned to Frank and said: 'I won't be able to come with you when they pick you up. I have a flatmate and if I don't show my face she may go to the police and say that I am missing.' Frank started to interrupt but she continued: 'She is bound to know that Reggie came to the club and took me somewhere. I couldn't even phone her, I had strict orders from Reggie not to get in touch with anybody. But I do promise, Frank, that when you get settled at Ronnie's friend's mansion, I will ask them if it is possible for me to come down and stay with you for a while.'

Frank looked very upset at Lisa's words. 'Will you marry me later? If everything goes well, even if I have to go back to prison?' he asked her.

'Of course, if that is what you want,' Lisa replied, and I knew she was only trying to humour him.

He seemed to accept her words and cheered up. He went into the bathroom and we could hear him cleaning his teeth yet again. While he was in the bathroom, Lisa, who was looking very worried, said to me: 'How am I going to get out of all this? I can't go with him. I have done everything they have asked me to do. Now that they are coming to take him away tonight I would like to go away and forget I was ever here.'

I tried to keep her calm and said, 'You will have to be like me and stick it out until Ronnie comes to pick him up.'

At last we all got to bed – it was five in the morning. I didn't leave after all – I did as Frank asked, and I stayed. About one hour later, Frank came into my bedroom. I was still sitting on the bed smoking and wondering what they could have planned for Frank. I knew that it was all lies about Ronnie coming over to the flat. He would say anything to keep things going the way he planned.

'What's the matter?' I asked him. 'Can't you sleep either?'

'No, I can't,' he answered. 'If they are going to pick me up tonight, I would like to take a chance and go round to see my family.'

I felt a shock run through me at his words. I had to talk him out of it. 'I don't think that would be a very good idea,' I told him. 'The cops are bound to be looking for you and they would most likely be hanging about where your family lives, ready to pounce, and you will muck up all the plans the twins have made.'

His attitude changed. 'All right, all right,' he said, 'but I still want Lisa to go with me.'

'I will ask them – that's all I can do,' I said. I was starting to get irritated by his persistence, and I was also very tired. 'Why don't you go and have a few more hours in bed with Lisa? The time will pass quicker for you,' I told him.

Just then Lennie came into the room with a cup of tea. 'I can't sleep,' he said, 'so I am going to make some breakfast. Shall I bring some into you and Lisa?' he asked Frank.

'No,' he replied, 'let her sleep, we will have it later,' and he went back to his bedroom.

I told Lennie that I would come into the kitchen and keep him company. He had a concerned look on his face. 'What's going to happen to Frank?' he asked. 'Do you really think they are going to get him out of the country?' He carried on, 'You know as well as I do that he is just like a child – someone would have to be with him at all times. I will be glad when tonight is over, I haven't had any sleep for about ten days.'

'How did you get involved in all this?' I asked.

'Oh,' he replied, 'Charlie knew that I lived alone and he asked me if I could do the firm a favour.'

'Have you had any money from them yet?' I asked.

'Only the few quid for food,' he said. 'I am supposed to get paid off tonight.'

'I wish you luck,' I commented. I knew that he wouldn't get paid for this favour. No one ever did – all they got were promises. Any money that was coming into the firm would be used to keep Ronnie at his hide-out and Frank at his.

The last day seemed to drag. At about three in the afternoon Albert came to the flat. Albert was another member of the firm. He was Irish and stood about six-foot tall. He was broad and fair-looking. He and I often used to drink together, and we got on well. Once he and Reggie had had a huge row in a pub which ended up with Albert being shot in the foot by Reggie. After that he had become Reggie's right-hand man for a while – until he fell from favour.

Now he took Frank into the bedroom to tell him the details about where he would be going. They were in there about fifteen minutes – it was obvious to me that he didn't want us to know what he was saying.

Frank came out of the bedroom looking excited. 'He is really coming over here for me tonight, Albert just told me, and he has said that Lisa can come with me.'

I glanced over at Lisa and she still looked scared as he raved on about what his plans were going to be, so I gave her the nod to take him back into the bedroom. When they had closed the door behind them, I turned to Albert. 'He is not really coming over to the flat to see Frank is he?' I asked.

'No,' he replied. 'They have told me just to humour him until he gets picked up tonight.'

'Who is coming for him and where are they going to take him?' I asked – knowing he wouldn't tell me but hoping anyway.

'You know that I can't tell you any details,' he answered. 'If they found out that I had told any of you about their plans I would be in a lot of bother. It's better that you don't keep asking questions – that way you will keep out of trouble with them.'

As he was talking I started to get the same apprehensive feeling that I had got with Reggie the night before. 'I am not a fool, Albert,' I told him. 'I smell a rat. We are all in this very deep and sooner or later we are all going to end up nicked – down to the twins.'

We were both silent for a minute and he handed me a cigarette. Then I remembered something. 'Frank wants to take a chance and go round to see his family. He has been driving me round the bend, and if he wants to go I can't stop him. I don't think anybody else could stop him either.'

'He can't go out,' Albert said. 'If he goes there and gets picked up by the law, we will all be in it up to our necks.'

He asked if there was any drink in the flat – he was getting irritable with me now. I passed him a large scotch and he carried on talking. 'They are depending on you to keep him here. They know you can handle him.'

I poured myself a drink and said, 'I don't know how I got involved in looking after a stranger for ten days. It was only supposed to be for forty-eight hours. I must have been off my head to agree. Roll on tonight. With any luck I should be on my way up North for New Year. When you go back, tell them that I am definitely not going to the country with Frank. I think I have stuck it out long enough. You can tell them to let someone else have a go at looking after him – I feel like a babysitter.'

'It will all be over tonight, and there is nothing else I can tell you,' he said. 'And for your own sake, don't ask any more questions – you know I have already been shot in the foot by Reggie and I sure don't want a bullet in the head – so just leave it out.'

I shut up then because I knew Albert was doing his best not to get me further involved.

He called out to Frank, who was still in the bedroom, 'I am going now, Frank. See you tonight. Be ready at seven – Ronnie doesn't like to be kept waiting.'

Frank came out saying, 'All right, all right. I'll be ready.' His face was flushed with excitement.

As Albert was leaving, I thought he had a strange look on his face that I had not seen before. When the door closed behind him, Lennie, who had been in the kitchen, called out that dinner was ready. At about six o'clock, Frank went into the front bedroom to look out of the window. He was in there for about a minute when he came out shouting: 'There are police outside.' He thought that the place was surrounded, but it was only a couple of uniform police walking past. Frank had almost jumped out of the back window – and this was only an hour before he was to be picked up. When he had calmed down Lisa said, 'You had better get yourself dressed in your new shirt and jeans that Lennie got for you. You want to look smart when Ronnie comes to pick you up.'

Frank nodded in agreement. Although he was a big man, he was very simple-minded. He went to get ready and when he came out of the bedroom he really looked good in his new clothes. While we were all hanging about waiting for the time to pass, the phone rang twice and we all knew that they were now on their way. It wasn't a long wait. At five minutes to seven, there was the usual secret knock on the front door. Lennie went to open it and Albert was standing there. He walked into the living room where we were all waiting. He didn't look at Frank for a while and the atmosphere seemed cool. Then he said: 'It's time, Frank. Ronnie won't be coming in, he is waiting in the van outside.'

Frank looked very disappointed. 'I thought that he was coming over in a car for me,' he said, looking puzzled.

Albert looked a bit tense. 'He thinks it would be better to leave London in the van,' he said, 'then get picked up by car.'

Frank looked pleased at Albert's words and said, 'Yes, what a good idea, he always thinks of everything.'

He turned to Lisa, who was standing in the background not really paying much attention to what they were saying. 'Come on, Lisa, get your things. You might as well come with me now – they must have room in the van for both of us.'

Lisa looked at me for support, with fear in her eyes, and said, 'Not yet, Frank. I will get them to bring me to you later when you get settled in to wherever you are going.'

Albert then interrupted, and smiled at him. 'She will be with you in the next few days, Frank. Don't worry – you know she loves you.'

Frank looked stubborn and I thought he definitely was not going to leave without Lisa. Albert pulled him to one side. 'Come on,' he said, worried now because Frank seemed determined not to leave. 'You don't want to keep Ronnie waiting. You know he has got to get out of London himself. He has been like you, cooped up in a flat in Finchley – and he has been there for weeks.'

While they were talking, Lisa came up to me and whispered: 'I don't want to go. Help me, please.'

I looked at Albert, and I could see he was getting anxious. 'Frank,' he said, 'I will find out where you are going and I will have her with you in twenty-four hours. She must let her flatmate know where she is going. Please trust me,' he continued. 'Come on, let's go now, he is waiting.'

While they were arguing about Lisa, Lennie went into the bedroom to make sure Frank hadn't left anything behind, and I looked at Lisa reassuringly, but it seemed ages before Frank finally agreed to leave without Lisa. As we were all shaking hands Lennie hurried out of the bedroom to wish him luck. Frank stood for a long time, kissing his newfound love, while we stood by awkwardly.

As he walked out of the door with Albert, he looked very sad. I knew it was because Lisa was staying behind, but we all sighed with relief – it had been a very tense few minutes and we were rather pleased that he had left peacefully without any more fuss. Lennie, Lisa and myself stood looking at each other for a couple of minutes when suddenly we heard what sounded like three gunshots.

Lisa was the first to react and she screamed out hysterically: 'They have shot him! Oh God, they have shot him!'

The colour drained from her face, and Lennie and I stood frozen. Then we heard another two shots. Lisa, still hysterical, wanted to open the door and run out into the street to see if her worst fears were confirmed.

I caught hold of her and said, 'Don't go out for Chrissake! If they have shot him and you see them you will be next. You don't want to be an eyewitness do you?'

Lennie tried to play it down to calm Lisa. 'I don't think it was gunshots,' he said, looking hopeful. 'It sounded more like a car backfiring.'

I looked at him, not quite so hopeful. 'I hope you are right,' I said, 'for all our sakes.'

As we stood there, wondering what had happened outside, there was a knock on the street door. We weren't expecting anybody, and Lisa started to shake. Before Lennie opened the door, I whispered to Lisa: 'For God's sake, don't go with anybody unless you know them, if they ask you to.'

She was shaking so much that I went over to the drinks cabinet and got her a drink. I put it in her hand and said: 'Here, drink this, it will stop you from shaking.'

I had a quick one myself because by then I was fearing the worst.

Lennie had opened the street door and two members of the firm came in very quickly. They looked at the three of us and the look on their faces confirmed the truth. Something terrible had happened. I wondered then whether somebody outside in the van had shot Frank, so I asked them: 'What has happened to Frank?'

One of them replied: 'Don't ask fucking questions. We have had orders to take the girl to the pub and you have got to stay with Lennie and clean this place up.' His voice was full of panic. 'Make sure that there is nothing left here belonging to Mitchell.'

I nodded, and remembered that Frank had given Lisa a comb. It was a small gift that he had wanted her to have. I thought, 'Poor bastard. He had such high hopes and had been so full of life.' In my mind, I knew they must have shot him – but I just couldn't fathom out why. After all, in the last ten days I had got to know him very well and he seemed to be the type of man who would give himself up without trouble if asked to by Ronnie. The worst that could have happened to Bill, Lennie and myself if Frank had gone back to prison and talked to the police was that we would have been charged with harbouring an escaped prisoner.

Lisa still looked nervous and said: 'I don't want to go to a pub. I can phone for a taxi from here and go home. This has all been a terrible nightmare for me and I just want to forget I was ever here.' She was very near to tears now, and it was obvious to me that she was still thinking about Frank and the shots that we all had heard.

'You have got to come with us,' one of them told her. 'There is some money over at the pub for you and they are having a party. Anyway, Reggie wants you there.'

I put my arm round her shoulders and said: 'Don't worry, you will be all right. I will see you over there later.'

Lennie had been looking out of the window, and he came over and said: 'The van's gone.' But there was no comment from the two men.

Lisa asked them to wait a few minutes while she packed some things that she had brought with her. When she came out of the bedroom she said goodbye to Lennie and me.

As they were leaving, one of the men turned to me and said: 'When you have finished here, you have got to come over to the pub.'

I nodded but made no comment.

Lennie and I cleaned up the flat and sat talking about the events of the last ten days. 'Do you think they really shot poor Frank?' asked Lennie.

I thought for a moment. 'I don't know,' I replied. 'It did sound like gunshots to me, but I don't think you should start asking questions. If I were you, I would go back to work on my stall and try to forget all that has happened. But be careful who you talk to. If anybody thinks that you are trying to find out what happened to Frank, you and Lisa could go the same way.' I got up to leave.

'Will I see you again?' he asked.

'No,' I replied, 'I don't think so. But someone will be in touch.'

We shook hands. 'Be lucky,' I said, and left the flat door for the last time.

I never did see Lennie again.

CHAPTER 11

WHO KILLED FRANK?

My last orders had been to go to the pub, but I didn't feel like drinking with the firm knowing in my heart that they had Mitchell shot for no reason. 'Poor Frank,' I thought, 'you would have been better off if you had never escaped from Dartmoor Prison.'

It was about 9.30, so I went home to my own flat and I stayed away from the firm for about two days. I knew they wouldn't miss me because it was Christmas and there were a lot of parties going on.

The first member of the firm I saw was Ian. He came round to my flat to see me.

'Where the hell have you been?' he asked. 'You were supposed to come to the pub for the Christmas party – Reggie gave strict orders for all the firm to be there.'

'Fuck the parties! We are all going to do plenty of bird for nothing – or some of us are going to end up dead,' I shouted at Ian. Then I quietened down a bit and poured us both a drink. 'It's nearly New Year and you did say you were coming up to Scotland with me. What's changed your mind?' I said.

He gulped his drink in one swallow. 'I have got a message,' he said, handing me his glass for a refill. 'Ronnie says he doesn't want you to leave London. You are to go over to the flat in Finchley. I had better mark your card – he knows you haven't been available since you left Lennie's and he wants to have a talk with you.'

I started to get on edge. 'I'm not in the mood to go over there,' I said.

'You had better go or they will think you are trying to get out,' he said, 'and you know what he gets like when he is moody.'

I looked Ian straight in the eye and asked: 'Did you know that they shot the Mad Axeman? After getting him out of prison and promising to get him a release date.'

'It wasn't Ronnie,' he said, 'I was with him in the flat when he told Albert to pick him up.'

'Then he must have ordered it,' I remarked, 'because we all heard the shots. Who will be next on the list? It's getting out of hand. Look what's happened in the past year – you get involved in the Cornell shooting; Jimmy from the club in North London got shot in the foot, for nothing; Nobby, Charlie's pal, got shot in the leg; and, before our time, Albert got shot in the foot.'

Ian looked startled when I mentioned Albert getting shot. 'How did you know about Albert?' he asked.

'Oh,' I answered, 'it was mentioned around the firm, but I know now the minor extent to which he was involved with Mitchell's shooting.'

Ian was looking thoughtful, and I carried on talking. 'Who is next on the list? It could be one of us.'

He agreed with everything I was saying. 'Between you and me,' he said, 'we are in very deep now. They are so powerful, they have got people who would do anything for a price.'

He got up to leave, and I told him I would go and have a talk with Ronnie, later.

It was all over the East End that Frank Mitchell had been shot. Everybody was talking about it and the police had been making extensive enquiries – but they had come up against the wall of silence and nobody had been arrested. Before I left to go to Finchley, I decided to write a letter to one of my brothers in Scotland, telling him that if I didn't keep in touch he was to give the sealed envelope inside to the police. The envelope contained some details about the Cornell murder and Frank Mitchell's disappearance that I thought would be useful to them if anything were to happen to me.

I got dressed and drove over to see Ronnie. He answered the door himself, which was very unusual. Normally somebody else opened the street door.

I looked around when I walked in. 'Why are you on your own?' I asked him. 'Where's Teddy?'

Knowing that Teddy had been with Ronnie for the last ten days, I had expected to see him now.

Ronnie gave me one of his weird smiles and, lighting up a cigarette, said: 'He has gone on a trip out of the country and he won't be back for a while.' Then he changed the subject and said, 'Why didn't you go to the Christmas party at the pub? You were told to go after you left Lennie's flat.'

I decided that I also needed a cigarette, and I poured myself a drink – both were always very plentiful. Then I said: 'I wasn't in the mood for any parties. I just fancied having a few drinks with a friend of mine.'

That was the worst thing I could have said. He seemed to explode and go red in the face. 'What friend?' he shouted. 'Do I know him? Where does he come from?'

I had to think fast. I couldn't tell him who he was because he was in the police force and I had known him quite a while.

'No, you don't know him. I used to work for him in his car hire business and I sometimes have a drink with him.'

He seemed to accept what I told him.

'Let's have another drink,' I said, and I poured him a gin and tonic, while I had a rum and coke. I could see that he was under some strain because he had been cooped up in that flat for over a month now.

'Did Mitchell leave anything at the flat?' he asked.

'No,' I replied, 'he took everything with him.'

I decided not to tell him about the comb that Lisa had kept, which was a gift from Frank. It would only have created more aggravation.

As we sat there drinking, he said: 'What about the girl? Will she keep her mouth shut if it gets around that Mitchell is down in the country?'

I could see that Ronnie was trying to convince me that Frank was still alive. 'It's all over the East End,' I said, 'that Frank Mitchell was shot dead.'

'We want people to think that,' he commented, 'so that the police will stop looking for him in the East End.' He carried on speaking. 'He is in a safe place and Teddy will be looking after him. They haven't seen anything in the newspapers yet about the letters they wrote.'

I had to be very careful how I asked my next question, but it was on my mind and had to be asked, and this seemed a good time to ask him, while we were on our own.

'Did Albert kill Frank, when he took him out to the van?'

Now that I had started, I had to continue. Before he had a chance to answer I carried on: 'I am only asking because we heard about five gunshots.'

He jumped up and seemed to lose control. 'He's fucking dead!' he shouted. 'We had to get rid of him – he would have got us all into a lot of trouble. We made a mistake getting that bastard out. He told Bill he was going round to Vallance Road – and no bastard goes to my mother's house unless I want him to.' He started to rave on. 'He has cost us about five grand and we have had to put others on promises. I suppose that little bookstall geezer will be looking for his five hundred now that it is all over – we will have to keep an eye on him.'

'I stayed at the flat with Lennie,' I said, 'for a couple of hours after they took Lisa away. He told me that he is going to try to get an exchange on his flat because he doesn't think he can stay there much longer.'

Ronnie butted in when he heard that. 'We will have to find out where he moves to just in case.' Then he repeated what he had said earlier: 'Do you think the girl can be trusted?'

I had no time to make any comment because he carried straight on: 'I never like the idea of getting him a bird – you can't trust them – she will have to be watched at all times.'

I disagreed. 'I don't think you will have to worry about the girl,' I said. 'Albert has been staying with her for the past two days. If he thought that she was going to talk, he would let you know.'

He lit a cigarette and sat staring at me. 'We should have let her go with that bastard Mitchell,' he said slowly. 'She would have been one less to worry about.'

I repeated what I had already said and then changed the subject. 'Is anybody coming over tonight to keep you company?'

I could see that he was getting depressed being cooped up in the flat for so long, and he would be worse now that Teddy had gone and he was alone. I never did see Teddy again. A few members of the firm asked about him in the days that followed, but they all got the same answer: 'He has gone to stay with Mitchell in the country.'

Ronnie poured us a drink and said, 'There is nobody coming over here tonight. Reggie has got things to do and we have been told that there is a tail on him. You had better stay here tonight, he should be over here in the morning.'

This didn't appeal to me at all. It was something I never expected him to ask. I knew it would be a boring evening but I couldn't refuse; he wasn't one for watching TV and the records he listened to were classical and not my scene. I left him sitting and smoking, very deeply in thought, at about one o'clock in the morning – but I couldn't sleep. I kept thinking about what he had said about Teddy being with Mitchell and getting rid of Lisa. If he could shoot someone in cold blood, he could do anything and probably get away with it.

I eventually dozed off, but I was awakened by the smell of gas in my bedroom. There was a gas fire in the room and it had been left with the gas open. I got up and turned it off. I didn't sleep at all after that – my mind was working overtime. Did Ronnie come in and turn it on? Or did I accidentally turn it on? I never found the answer to that.

Nor could I understand why Ronnie was still in hiding. There was no warrant out for his arrest and it was costing the firm quite a lot of money to keep him in the private flat. Ronnie hated being cooped up and not knowing what was going on and I knew that Reggie would not be able to handle things for long on his own as he didn't have the same command as his brother.

I was glad when it was morning and I got up early and cooked breakfast for the two of us. After a couple of hours, Reggie came over with one of the firm. He told us that he had to make a few detours on the way because he was sure the police had someone following him. Ronnie took this quite seriously and said to the minder who had come with Reggie, 'Go out and buy some cigarettes and have a good look round, just to make sure that nobody tailed you over here.'

There were only the three of us in the flat now, and Reggie turned to me, showing his annoyance, and said, 'I haven't seen you about for a few days – where have you been?'

Pointing to Ronnie, I said, 'I have already told him where I've been and what I've been doing.'

They were always so suspicious – they expected us all to account for every evening spent away from them.

Then I repeated what I had asked Ronnie. 'Is it true what everyone in the East End is saying, that Mitchell is dead?' I wanted to hear it from them both, then I would know that it was true.

Flushing, Reggie looked straight at me and answered: 'Yes. It was a big mistake getting him out of prison, we should have left him there. He has been a big burden to us and has cost us a fortune. We still have to find more money to pay off a few people to keep their mouths shut.'

At these words Ronnie looked furious. 'We are not paying anybody anything. We have paid enough – they can go to hell,' he said, raising his voice. 'Even if I have to give them a little help.' Again, he gave his funny smile.

The minder came back into the flat with the cigarettes and reported: 'There is no one about, I don't think we were followed over here.'

I was getting impatient to leave, so I said: 'You don't need me any more now so I will be going.'

I got up to leave and Ronnie said: 'Yes, go round to the clubs and see if there is a lot of talk about Mitchell. If anybody is making themselves busy asking too many questions you had better let us know. We will be in touch.'

I was glad I didn't have to stay there for another night, but I didn't bother going round the clubs, I just went straight back to my flat. In the evening I went round to my local pub, one that the rest of the firm never used. I had only been in there for about an hour when Jack the Hat walked in. By the look of him I could see that he had already been drinking somewhere else.

'Where is everyone?' he asked in his usual breezy way. 'I haven't seen the twins or any of the firm for days.'

I had to lie to him, knowing what a nuisance he could be when drunk: 'I haven't seen them either. I think they have gone down to the country.'

Jack didn't believe me. 'The bastards are in hiding,' he said aggressively. 'Everybody is saying that they have killed one of my best friends, Big Frank. The dirty bastards – they should be castrated.'

He carried on rambling and his voice was getting so loud I had to tell him to shut up, but he said: 'Frank was a great friend of mine, one day they will get their lot, and no one will miss them.'

I listened to all this because I liked him. Ian and I treated him as a friend even though he was a bit of a drunk.

'I don't know why you and I stay with the firm,' he continued. 'If they can do that to one of their friends, they can do it to you.'

There was a lot of truth in what he was saying, but I didn't answer. One day, if he wasn't careful about the way he kept shooting his mouth off, he was going to land himself in big trouble. Unfortunately he wasn't a man to take advice although many people tried to steer him on the right course.

'Do you want to come to the Regency Club with me for a drink?' Jack asked me.

'No, not tonight,' I answered. He was the last person I would go drinking with – he seemed to attract trouble wherever he went. To shake him off I said I had a meeting with the rest of the firm and I stood up to leave.

'I will be in touch,' I said as I left and drove home.

The next afternoon I went round to Bill's house. He was pleased to see me and asked me in. There was no one else in the house so I asked him if he would like to come out and have a quiet drink and a chat. I wanted to find out whether he knew more about Mitchell than I did.

'Yes, I would,' he replied. 'As a matter of fact there are a few things I want to ask you about Big Frank.'

We went to a quiet pub that none of the firm used

and after we had got our drinks we sat at a corner table, which was quite secluded, Bill started talking. 'Is it true,' he asked, 'that Big Frank is really dead? I haven't slept for days knowing that I was looking after him only a week ago.'

I didn't have to answer that question because he already knew the answer, but wanted me to confirm it.

'Why did this have to happen?' he asked. 'You know as well as I do that he was harmless. He wouldn't have done anything to get the firm into any trouble. I am telling you this as a friend – if I ever get picked up I am not getting involved with his murder.'

I nodded and said: 'I agree with you, Bill, but do you really think you can walk away from the past few weeks and live to tell the tale?'

I could talk to him like this because we had a mutual trust in each other. He was very worried and looked it.

'Do you know where I can get in touch with Ronnie?' he asked. 'I would like to have a talk with him.'

I knew it was out of the question taking him to Ronnie's flat in Finchley because very few people knew about it, so I said: 'He will be coming out of hiding in the next few days. I don't think you should say anything to him about Mitchell, or ask any questions – it's a very sore point with him at the moment.'

I lit myself a cigarette and Bill refused mine saying that he preferred to roll his own. I continued the conversation: 'I would keep out of the way if I were you. It can't be too long before someone talks to the police. They are not fools, they have been keeping out of our way, and we haven't even seen the local ones who drink where we drink. Let's face it, if all the East End are saying that Frank was killed, then the police must be doing something about it. I will keep in touch with you. Don't worry, I will let you know what's going on.'

Once again Ronnie came out of hiding and things got back to normal, with members of the firm going round the clubs collecting their protection money. There was talk at one of the meetings about building up an arsenal of guns. Word had gone around that there were some people about who wanted revenge over Mitchell's disappearance. Once again, I was sent for by Ronnie, and he said: 'I want you to go over to the cinema in Edmonton. I have made arrangements for the Yank to meet you there and he will give you a parcel. Take it round to Pat's place and tell him to store it.'

I got into my car and drove across London to

Edmonton in North London. I got there early, and remembering what Reggie had said a few months before, I had a stroll around making sure there were no police traps. Reggie had never trusted the Yank. When he arrived, he didn't get out of the car but beckoned me to follow him. We drove to a quiet road in Tottenham, where we pulled up. He handed over the parcel, which I put in the boot of my car, and he drove away.

I hadn't been told what was in the parcel, but from the weight of it I presumed it was the guns. I took them round to Big Pat's place as I was asked. He was waiting for me and when he took the parcel in he opened it and stood back, shocked. Then he said: 'For Christ's sake. What are they going to do with them? Is there going to be a war?' He was referring to what was now on show to us. Two 1948 Bren guns with ammunition. They were like the ones I had used in the Royal Marine Commandos.

'Don't worry,' I told him, smiling to myself. 'They will never be used. Ronnie just likes to have guns around. You should know, you've been with the firm long enough.'

Pat wasn't so sure, and he said, 'People don't buy guns unless they intend to use them.'

He picked up the parcel, which he had re-wrapped,

and started to walk across the room. But I stopped him and said: 'I don't want to know where you keep your arsenal. I am going back now to tell them that I have delivered them to you.'

I walked to the door. 'See you later,' I called out, and left. I drove back to the pub and, as I walked in, I saw Reggie and Ronnie talking to some of the firm. Ronnie came straight over to me and, putting his hand on my shoulder, whispered, 'Well, did you see the Yank?'

'Yes,' I replied, 'I have picked the parcel up and delivered it to where you told me.'

I didn't tell him that I had seen what was in it. I just wanted to forget about it and hope the guns were never used. Frank Mitchell was still uppermost in my mind. I knew I wouldn't rest until I found out what really had happened to him. There was only one man who could tell me the truth if I managed to get him in the right frame of mind. That man was Albert.

I decided to ask him one evening when most of the firm had gone to one of the West End nightspots. Albert and I met for a drink in a club in North London. After we had settled at the usual corner table I asked him: 'What did happen when you took Mitchell out to that van? Did you have orders to get rid of him?'

He started to look a bit cagey and I said: 'Don't worry, I only want to know for my own satisfaction. I have been hearing so many different stories since the night you walked out of the flat with him.'

I lit up a cigarette and went over to the bar for drinks, leaving Albert to chew over my words. When I got back to the table I carried on speaking. 'You are the only one who holds the key. He was done in, wasn't he? We all heard the shots, even Lisa must have told you when you were sleeping with her. Did you tell them that she was scared now?'

'No,' he replied, 'of course I didn't. I wouldn't want anything to happen to her. She has only done what she was asked and I think she would be frightened to say anything about it.'

No matter how persuasive I was, he didn't intend to tell me who he thought shot Mitchell. As he got up to go to the Gents, I thought, 'I had better not press it any further just in case it got back that I was quizzing him.'

We didn't discuss Frank any more and after an hour or so, I got up to leave. The following morning I went round to Ian's flat. He looked as though he had a giant-sized hangover.

'Where did you all go last night?' I asked.

'We went to the West End,' he answered, 'and

we all had a ball. But they started screaming at each other.'

I got interested. 'What was it about this time?' I asked, knowing that it was the usual thing to happen when they were out drinking together.

Ian replied: 'They were talking about a geezer called Payne. Ronnie told Reggie that he wants him bumped off. He has heard from some associates of his that Payne has been to the law. They seem to be worried about this one.'

'I don't know anything about Payne,' I said. 'I have only heard that he did some deals with the twins before our time. I remember taking Reggie to his solicitor's office in Fleet Street to meet Payne but he didn't show up. Who's got the job of bumping him off?'

Ian laughed as he said, 'They are talking about getting Jack the Hat to do it. They even said that they would let him off with that double-cross on the last job he did for the firm with Nobby's merchandise.'

I couldn't believe this and said so. 'They have got to be joking. Jack's no assassin – he is only a small-time crook. Why should he put himself out on a limb for them? He's not on the firm and if anything went wrong he would be on his own.'

'Well,' said Ian, 'they still want him to do this favour for them.'

I laughed and said, 'I wish them luck.'

We found out later that they eventually tracked down Jack the Hat and told him that they would forget about the past if he would do them this favour. He agreed immediately because he was eager to get back into their good books. He was taken to the area where Payne lived so that he could 'case the joint'. After he had looked round the area and made mental notes about the house, he got back into the car that had taken him and said: 'After you drop me off, go back and tell them it's as good as done.'

Once again he was given his expenses for the job in advance, but one or two of us knew that he had no intention of shooting anybody for £100. He would agree to anything as long as he had his drinking money, even if it meant double-crossing the twins once again. I didn't care who they asked to do these kind of favours, as long as it wasn't me.

We waited a few days for news that he had done what he was paid to do, because this time the twins were sure he wouldn't let them down. To safeguard themselves they even held parties and meetings to make sure they had alibis for when the event took place. But some of the firm had been right. Jack didn't do the job, but he did spend the money and, true to form, dropped out of sight. The cards were now stacked up against Jack the Hat. Some of us knew that he couldn't possibly get away with it.

CHAPTER 12

SOME NOSY PARKERS AND THE MAFIA

One evening, Ronnie decided to hold a party in one of his favourite haunts, a pub called the Old Horns in Warner Place, Bethnal Green. He told all the firm to bring their wives or girlfriends along because he had some showbusiness people coming and Reggie wanted to show off his new girlfriend. The guests of honour were two well-known American dancers – the Clark Brothers – who had their own dancing school in Tottenham Court Road, a blind pianist called Lennie Peters, and the well-known London photographer, David Bailey.

Everybody appeared to have forgotten about the shootings that had taken place and it seemed to us that the police were still not bothering with the firm's activities.

There were a lot of photos being taken that night by the firm's photographer, but during the evening I spotted a man standing at the bar alone. He was tall and thin, and he wasn't with the celebrities or the firm. He just kept on clicking away with his camera at all and sundry. I saw one of the firm go over to him to find out who he was. He reached into his pocket and took out a card which he showed, and said he was from a local newspaper, sent to photograph the celebrities that were there.

The member of the firm walked over to where Ronnie was sitting with the Americans. He bent down and whispered something to him. Ronnie looked up, but as this was going on the man suddenly left. Someone ran out of the pub to get the car number, but it was too late. The car was already receding into the distance.

Whispers started going round the pub that he was a plain-clothes man taking everybody's photo in the bar. But by now quite a lot of us were getting into the swing of things. The entertainment had been good and the entertainers were getting ready to leave. It looked as though it was going to be a trouble-free night, without anybody getting beaten up or having a bottle put in their face. And well it might have been, but for two strangers who walked in.

They came to the side of the bar where the firm were drinking and gave their order to the barman. The atmosphere suddenly changed and we all sensed trouble. The two dancers had already left and the other celebrities were on their way out. Ronnie had got up from the table where he had been sitting all evening. After saying goodbye to the last of his showbiz friends, he made his way over to the bar and said to the two strangers: 'This part of the bar is private. You will have to go round to the other side of the bar if you want to drink here.'

He was speaking very quietly, but I knew what was going to happen, we all did. After all, hadn't we seen it time and time again?

The two men looked at Ronnie and one of them said: 'We have already bought our drinks and nobody told us we can't drink here.'

It was obvious that they didn't know who Ronnie was or what his capabilities were.

Reggie moved towards his brother, and then it happened. The two strangers were taken by surprise as they were punched and kicked by Ronnie and Reggie, who didn't need any help, but a couple of the firm joined in. There were shouts from Ronnie that the men were spies from South London. The fight lasted for about ten minutes, then the twins stopped as suddenly as they started, and we got the two men, who were by now bleeding quite a lot, into a car and driven to the London Hospital.

Ronnie and Reggie went into the Gents to clean themselves up. As the door closed behind them, Jack the Hat popped his head into the bar. Ian was the first to see him. 'For Christ's sake,' he shouted, 'look who's at the door. If he comes in there will be trouble.'

I made a move towards the door. 'Don't say anything to them,' I said, meaning the twins. 'I will get rid of him.' I went outside to where Jack was standing. He was doped up as usual.

'I want to see the twins,' he said. 'I went round to that geezer Payne's house to shoot him but I think he has the law with him. There's nothing I can do now. I have the gun that they gave me – I want to give it back.' He took the gun out of his pocket. 'See,' he said, waving it about, 'I haven't fired it!'

I couldn't believe this was happening. 'Jack,' I said, 'there has been some bother here tonight and we are expecting the law round at any moment. If you get picked up with that gun you will get nicked, and the twins wouldn't like that. We have got to leave now and I think you should have it away sharpish. I will tell them what you have told me, but not until the morning.'

I knew that I couldn't tell them right now about Jack because the evenings were not the best times to give them bad news, especially after a bout of drinking.

'Go over to the Regency Club and I will try to see you there later,' I told him.

When I went back into the bar, I saw that everything had been cleaned up and the firm was ready to leave. I went over to Ian and said: 'I gave him a tenner to get rid of him,' which, in fact, I *had* done many times in the past.

Reggie came out of the Gents where he had been cleaning the blood off his hands. 'Is everything clear outside?' he asked.

'Yes,' someone answered, 'there doesn't seem to be any Old Bill about.'

I didn't tell him that Jack the Hat had been to the pub to speak to them. Reggie called across to the girl that he had brought with him. She was sitting with the other girlfriends and wives. They all looked slightly dazed at what had happened.

'We are leaving now, come on,' he said to her. Then he said to me, 'Come round to the house at twelve o'clock tomorrow. I have something to tell you.'

When they had left, the rest of the firm followed, but I decided to take my girlfriend to somewhere away from the others. The barman looked relieved to see us all go. If that photographer who we thought was the law hadn't left the pub so hurriedly, he would have had some real action photos.

The next morning I went round to the house as I had been asked. Nothing was said about what had happened the night before in the pub. It was almost as if it had never taken place. Ronnie was waiting for me when I arrived, and he had a grim look on his face.

'We have been told through the grapevine that a big Irishman has been going around the East End asking a lot of questions about us,' he said, and I must have looked startled because he went on, 'I don't know if it is anything to worry about, but I do want everybody to be on their guard.'

We found out later that it *was* something to worry about because this man was one of the 'top cops' in the police force.

As Ronnie finished speaking, Reggie came into the room where we were sitting and smoking. He was dressed very smartly, as usual, and he was sporting a pair of bruised knuckles from the fracas the night before.

'Ronnie and I are going to Tottenham Court Road,' he told me, 'and we want you to drive us there. We are borrowing the office of those two Yanks to do a bit of business in.'

The Yanks that he referred to were the two dancers from the night before.

'We have a meeting with a couple of members of the Mafia,' Ronnie said. He stood up, ready to leave, and Reggie and I followed suit.

His words came as no surprise to me. There had already been a few meetings with some of the top men from America who I thought had connections with the Mafia (I assumed they were gangsters).

As we left the house we saw two men sitting in a red Ford Cortina. I knew they were going to follow us, but we couldn't be sure whether they were the law or friends of the two men who had been badly beaten up in the pub. The twins didn't agree often, but this time they decided that the two men in the red car were the law. After all, there had been two murders and two shootings, apart from other smaller crimes, so it would seem obvious that the police would be trying to put evidence together.

I was told to drive around and try to lose them,

but it wasn't easy. They stuck to us like glue. However, after a while, I managed to shake them off in the heavy East End traffic and drive to the West End. I was instructed to park about two hundred yards from the office and we walked from the car to the building where the meeting was to be held, in what looked to me like a very high-class dancing academy. We were greeted by one of the brothers.

'Hello, Ron. Hello, Reg,' he smiled – but behind the smile was an air of unease. He led us upstairs to a very large office that was thickly carpeted and boasted a cocktail cabinet fully stocked with every kind of drink. It was the glamorous kind of office one would see in Hollywood films. I guessed that this was all to impress the Mafia.

Before they arrived, I was told by Ronnie not to speak but to stand by the door and just observe. After about twenty minutes there was a tap on the door and the American dancer called out: 'Your guests have arrived. If you need me I will be downstairs.' He then showed in two Italian-looking men. It was obvious that he didn't want to know what the meeting was about because he left the room immediately.

As the door closed behind him, both Ronnie and Reggie went over and shook hands with them. I recognised one of them right away – he had been at a flat we borrowed once in Albion Road, Stoke Newington, only a few months before. He turned to me and said, 'How are you? Long time no see.'

I shook hands with him and replied smilingly, 'I'm all right. I see you are still as fat as ever.'

He nodded and laughed. When I first met him I was told that he had been one of the bodyguards of a well-known American singer.

There was nothing very different about this meeting from previous ones. They talked and we listened. We looked like any normal businessmen in our pinstriped suits. The general idea was that the Mafia wanted to move in on London with the backing of various London gangs, and a few of their big shots were of the opinion that the firm could be of use to them. This was not the firm's style – taking orders from people from America. I could never imagine them taking orders from anybody – not even the Mafia. Though the twins agreed to nearly everything that was said.

I gathered that the man doing the talking was the spokesman. He was the one I had met before. He said that he was paving the way for another meeting with someone else who would be coming over to this country soon. We wouldn't be seeing him again because he was going back to the States that night. He pointed to the other man, who was also just observing, and said: 'He has booked a suite at a hotel near Hyde Park where you will be having the meet.'

They all agreed to this other meeting taking place in a few days' time.

The fat man was full of bounce and very jolly, and after the discussion was over, we all relaxed and I poured drinks for everyone. We all shook hands when they got up to leave and, before opening the door, he turned round and said, 'Make sure you go on that meet. I will phone you if I come back to London.'

They left as quietly as they had arrived and we sat down with another drink. Ronnie then said, 'We should go to the next meeting.' He got up and went over to the window.

Reggie didn't look so sure. 'I think it will be a waste of time. It looks like they only want to use our name,' he replied.

As usual, Ronnie had the last word, so it was agreed that we go to the hotel and find out what they really wanted the firm to do.

There was a tap on the door and the American walked in. We all stood up, and Ronnie said: 'Thanks for letting us use your office.'

'That's all right,' he answered, 'that's what friends are for.' He looked relieved, now that we were ready to go. We left the building and walked to where we had parked the car. We looked around to see if the red Cortina had tracked us down, but there was no sign of it. We drove back to the East End without making any conversation. When we pulled up, we noticed a car parked across the road. This time we felt sure that it was the police and that there was a twenty-four-hour tail on us.

About a week later we went on the meet to see the men from America at the hotel where they were staying near Hyde Park. I was beginning to feel quite at home there now as there had been so many meets in it in the past. We were met in the foyer by the fat man's friend, whom we had been with a week earlier. He took us up in the lift to a suite on the tenth floor, which consisted of a sitting room, bedroom and bathroom. It must have cost a fortune, I thought, to stay in a place like this. There was a man waiting.

I looked at the two men, who were looking at us at the same time. They looked like the Mafia I had seen in films, but these were for real with their dark suits and gold rings, and I reckoned that they were carrying guns. We all stood looking at each other for what seemed like minutes, but were only seconds.

Just then, another man appeared from out of the bedroom. He looked as though he had just finished shaving – he was only wearing a string vest and trousers. He looked pleased to see us and as he walked over to where we were standing, he put out both his hands and said, 'Which one is Ronnie?'

After all the introductions were made, he phoned down to room service and ordered tea and sandwiches.

As he put the phone down, he said: 'Christ, it's so easy to get into this goddamn country.' He proceeded to tell us how he had dressed up as first officer on board a cargo ship and docked in at Southampton. 'But I will be catching a plane back,' he grinned. 'That boat was too damn slow.'

The waiter tapped at the door and came in with the teas. Maybe I was getting over-suspicious, but even he looked out of place. I was sure he was the law – it seemed to me that he wasn't doing things right, the way that waiters were supposed to. As he was leaving the room, the man in the string vest asked him to put a sign on the door so that we wouldn't be disturbed.

When we finished the tea and sandwiches, we settled down to business, with me taking the position of observer again. The other two men also watched and said nothing. All the talking was done by the man in the string vest, and it was on the same lines as the previous meet – about taking over London gaming clubs and arranging for planes to take London gamblers to Las Vegas and bring wealthy Americans to London.

I knew that this was already being done by other syndicates from the West End clubs (groups of businessmen who financed trips to and from New York for gambling purposes) and I didn't think that the firm would want any unnecessary violence through muscling in on other gangs' territories. We had had clashes in the past with others trying to muscle in on ours. The firm had had phone calls from clubs and casinos telling them that men had been calling on them for protection money and saying they had been sent by the Krays. When this happened, members of the firm were sent along to sit and wait for these individuals and give them 'a word of warning'. After that we had no more trouble.

Ronnie looked fascinated by the man who was talking, but I don't think he was taking much notice of what he was saying. Reggie, on the other hand, was different. On this meet he sat there smoking and taking every word in, but saying nothing. However, I think that even he was fascinated by the way this man was putting the proposition over.

When he had finished speaking, he looked from one to the other for any comments. Ronnie stood up and lit a cigarette. Then he looked straight at the man who had done all the talking and said: 'It all sounds very nice, but we will have to give it some thought. There is no hurry for this at the moment. We will give you an answer in a few weeks' time.'

The man looked surprised. He must have thought that he was going to get the firm involved straight away. 'That's all right,' he said, 'but I will be going back to the States very soon. Will you get in touch through him?' He indicated one of the other two men with him. 'He will let me know your answer.'

Ronnie and Reggie nodded in agreement.

The meet was now over, and again we relaxed. Drinks were ordered and we all smoked and chatted till they were sent up. When our glasses were empty we stood and shook hands. Then we left the hotel. The drive back from this meet was again in silence. I had got used to this because it was common knowledge among the members of the firm that the two brothers didn't tell us everything that was happening. There was no sign of a police tail this time but when we got to Vallance Road a red Cortina with two men in it was waiting on the corner. Ronnie got out of the car and walked over to them. We could hear him say something about joining us for a cup of tea. When he came back he said to Reggie and me: 'I told them we'd be in Marge's pub tonight.' Then he gave his weird smile. He presumed they were police.

They never let me know whether anything came of these meetings with the Mafia, or whether they made any deals. I did suspect that they made some kind of deal because they had a couple of more meets in the hotel when I wasn't with them and there did seem to be a bit of cash about, though that could have been from any of the pies that the firm had their finger in.

CHAPTER 13

THE KILLING OF JACK THE HAT

There was quite a lot of boasting going on in the firm that no matter what they did, nobody could touch them. They wouldn't have felt so secure had they known then that the police were building up quite a case against them!

It was about this time that Jack the Hat's name was brought up again in the pub one night. Somebody told the twins that he was still going around telling everybody who cared to listen that he worked for the firm and that he was with Reggie when he shot Jim in the foot. This didn't go down well with them.

A couple of nights later I popped into a pub on my way home from the club to see some friends of mine and have a couple of drinks with them. Only two people knew that I used this pub, they were Jack and Ian. It was about nine o'clock when Jack walked in and came over to me. He said, 'Can I have a word with you?'

'Sure you can,' I told him.

As usual, he had the glazed look of the pill taker. I took him over to a corner table.

'What's the matter, Jack?' I asked. 'You look worried.'

'No, I'm all right,' he answered, 'but I have just come from the Regency Club and I have heard a whisper that the twins are looking for me. I know I can trust you, have you heard anything?'

This was the first time I had seen Jack scared.

'I know they have the needle with you,' told him. 'They have been told through the grapevine that you have been shooting your mouth off.'

He started to get flustered, but I carried on talking.

'You are still going around shouting your mouth off that you know they got rid of Mitchell and you are also telling everybody that you still have the gun that Reggie shot Jimmy with. I know that is bothering them.'

He started to flare up. 'I don't care about those two bastards.' His voice rose, and I had to tell him to keep it down.

'From now on,' he said, 'I am carrying a double-barrelled shotgun with me when I go out at nights. I don't want to use it, but if I have to I will. There are a lot of crooks going around saying that the firm is giving the East End a bad name and taking liberties with people.'

'Yes, I know,' I told him patiently, 'but they are not saying as much as you are. They all know what the twins are capable of doing. Do yourself a favour and keep out of the way.'

He looked resentful for a moment, then he said with his usual bravado: 'I don't care. One day it will be me or them, and as I have told you before, I am tooled-up. If they try to take me I shall most probably take one of them with me.'

As he paused, the waitress came over to clear our glasses and take another order for drinks. She smiled at Jack and said, 'Hello, Jack, I see you're still wearing your hat.'

When she went away to get our drinks, I said to him: 'All I am telling you is to be careful what you are saying. There are a lot of people that will run to the firm with what you are saying to get in their good books. I wouldn't like to hear that you are on the missing list like a few others we know.'

As we finished speaking, Ian walked into the bar

and as he approached our table, I called over for another drink to be brought with our order. When the waitress put them on the table, Jack repeated to Ian what he had told me about being tooled-up.

'Don't take any notice of him,' I said to Ian, 'he is talking through drink again.'

After about half an hour, Ian told Jack that we had to go. We had a tough time shaking him off because he wanted to go with us. As usual, we had to give him a few quid, and then we left him in the pub. Ian and I went back to my flat.

I was taken by surprise when he started talking about the last three years with the firm.

'I wish to Christ I had never come down to London,' he said. 'Do you think the police are onto the firm?'

Ian was very quiet and looked a hard man. What with the scar on his face, a lot of people were slightly afraid of him. I often thought that was why Ronnie liked to have him around when he went to strange pubs for meets. He was obviously thick with Ronnie – but not out of choice. I thought he looked worried. I had seen a lot of changes in him since we joined the firm, and I knew that since the Cornell murder he had been drinking more and taking pills. He was obviously under pressure.

'There are a lot of rumours going around,' I said. 'I don't really think that the police are sleeping – too much has happened.' He nodded and I continued. 'Look how many of the firm are still around. If you can remember the first time we ever met them in the pub, they appeared to have an army round them. After the Cornell shooting a lot of the smart ones got out. I know some of them had to leave London, but they still got out. And what about the Mad Axeman? You know what happened to him. I can't understand how I let myself be talked into looking after a complete stranger. You never met him, did you?' I asked.

Ian shook his head, and I said bitterly, 'He was harmless and his life was taken away from him for no reason. Who will be next? It could be one of us. I don't think that the firm have as many friends as they had three years ago.'

We arranged a meet for the next day, and Ian left.

As the weeks passed and we went to our usual local haunts and West End nightspots, I noticed that people weren't so eager to drink in our company, although there were a few new faces wanting to get on the firm. These were mostly young up-and-coming villains. I remember thinking back to the time when Ian and I were asked to work for the twins. We were strangers to London and had never heard of the firm and didn't know what they were involved in. We just saw the lure of the nightlife.

I could never understand what the fascination of the firm was for men who were small-time crooks and wanting to join it. Perhaps they wanted to get into the big time. However, I was glad to see these new faces because it gave a few of us who wanted it a chance to get out slowly and get on with our lives away from the firm. It was easy to get in, too: all you had to do was be invited for a drink and, if Ronnie liked the look of you, you'd be put on the payroll and then, in exchange, you started collecting money from the card clubs.

Meanwhile, word spread around that the firm had forgiven Jack the Hat, and he started getting round his old haunts again.

One early evening when I was at the club playing cards, one of the firm came in and called me over to one side.

'Ronnie is having a party late tonight at blonde Carol's house,' he told me. 'He wants you to come, but he doesn't want anybody to bring their wives or girlfriends. He said he only wants a few of the firm there. We will all be going to the Regency and then on to the party.'

I knew the house in Evering Road, Stoke Newington, very well. The party was going to be in the basement flat which Carol lived in. The firm sometimes paid her to let them use it for parties. There were a few houses in the same street where the firm sometimes met for drinks, and I remembered going to Big Pat's house there a few months previously, to deliver the two Bren guns for him to store away.

I thought back to some of the other parties that I had been ordered to attend. They had been more like meetings – it was only different when the women were there. I said I wouldn't be there because I had already made arrangements to meet my girlfriend's family. This was a lie, but I had to think up an excuse fast. I was fed up being at their beck and call.

As he left me to report back to them, I stopped playing cards and walked out of the club just in case there was a phone call for me. I never heard from anybody the next day and forgot all about the party that I had missed. Then, a day later, Ian came round to my flat. As I let him in he seemed to be bursting with excitement.

'Have you heard?'

'Heard what?' I asked him, feeling puzzled.

He seemed to take a deep breath. 'Reggie and Hart have murdered Jack the Hat.'

I felt as though time stood still. I just stared at him in disbelief and then sat down to light a cigarette.

'What are you talking about?' I gasped. 'There was nothing in the papers about any murder. Are you sure?'

It took Ian a long time to convince me that Jack was dead. I found it hard to digest. Maybe he had got it wrong.

'Were you there when it happened?' I asked, clutching at straws.

'No, thank Christ,' he replied, 'I didn't go. I didn't want to leave Pat – we haven't been out for a few days.'

'Who told you about it then?' I asked him.

'I had to go to the East End last night and I saw Hart in the pub on his own,' he replied, 'and when he told me what had happened, I reacted just like you. I just couldn't believe what he was telling me. The way he was talking gave me the impression that he helped Reggie to stab him.'

Ronnie Hart had joined the firm when he came out of the army and was a good-looking guy – dark, tall and strong – who always boasted that he would do anything for Ronnie and Reggie – his cousins, although he used to call them his 'uncles'. He was always good company and lively, with a taste for excitement. Like the rest of us, he had originally been attracted by the glamour of the firm's nightlife – not the violence that went with it. I liked him.

Ian still looked a bit shocked by it all even as he told me.

'It looks as though Hart's got himself well involved now,' I told him, 'just like you are with Ronnie.' Then a thought struck me. 'I wonder why there is nothing in the papers about it,' I said.

Ian shook his head and said he didn't know. He started to say that it had happened at a party a few nights ago in Evering Road.

'Christ,' I broke in, 'that's the party they wanted me to go to.'

Ian started filling me in on the sordid details that Hart had told him the night before. It seemed that the party was in full swing when somebody said they were running out of booze. One young man, who was not a member of the firm but who had been invited along, was asked to go round to the Regency Club and get some more drink. He was also told to look around and see if there was anybody there that the firm knew. When he came back he said that Jack the Hat was there shouting his mouth off as usual. Ronnie heard this and told the young man and a new member of the firm to go back to the Regency Club and ask Jack to come for a drink. They were asked not to bring anyone else – only Jack the Hat.

I listened to this without interrupting, then I said: 'Are you sure that it was Reggie that stabbed Jack?'

'Yes,' he answered. 'Hart told me that he started to stab him with a kitchen knife during the party.'

'What happened after that?' I asked.

'They got two of the firm to put the body into a car and take it over to the other side of London,' Ian replied.

'Does Charlie know about it?' I asked.

'Yes,' he answered, 'Hart told me that Charlie was called out to arrange for the body to be taken care of.'

'I wonder what has happened to it,' I said slowly, thinking how my good advice had fallen on deaf ears.

'I don't know,' said Ian, 'but my guess is that it's been cremated.'

'Do you know where Ronnie and Reggie are now?' I asked.

'No, I don't,' he answered.

We both sat thinking for a few minutes, then I turned to him and said: 'So far, none of the firm knows where either of us lives. If they have been looking for us or have tried to get in touch, they wouldn't know where to start. I want to keep it that way. You are the only one who knows my address and I want you to keep it to yourself. After what happened to Jack I don't want any late calls to any parties.'

'Nothing will happen,' he said, 'and they will get out of this – remember that they know a few influential people.'

I looked at him and thought how different he was since Ronnie had taken him on as his right-hand man. He really thought that nothing could touch the twins.

Ian said that Hart had told him we should all stay away from the twins' mother's place for a while. He got up to leave and I offered him a lift. I told him I was going over to the club to try to find out who was at that party. He looked at me but said nothing.

The first person I contacted was a young man called Tony. I had only met him a few weeks before. He was a likeable man, married with two children, and he enjoyed being in the firm's company. He greeted me with the same story that I had heard from Ian that morning. Jack the Hat was dead.

'How did you know?' I asked.

'I was there,' he told me.

It turned out he was the one who had fetched Jack from the Regency Club.

'What the fuck did you want to get mixed up with the firm for? You're a married man and you go to work,' I said.

He was beginning to look a bit green. 'I didn't know that they wanted him at the party to kill him,' he said. 'I would never have gone and asked him to come there had I known what was going to happen. Poor Jack, he never had a chance. He even tried to jump out of the window on to the path. They tried to shoot him at first but the gun didn't go off.'

He paused for a moment, then I said: 'I liked Jack, I have known him for a long time. If I were you I wouldn't go around telling everyone that you were there. He may have had a big mouth, but he did have a lot of friends. And if they can't get at the twins they might sort out somebody else who was at that flat when it happened.'

He looked as though he was going to be sick. 'I didn't know they were going to kill him,' he repeated miserably.

Another day passed and there had been no word from Reggie or Ronnie. Once again they had decided to go missing for a couple of days till the gossip died down. However, they did send a message for us all to keep away from Carol's house. By now it was all over the clubs that there had been another murder –

and this time everyone was saying Reggie and Hart had done it. Some gamblers were even taking bets on whether or not the twins would be arrested before very long. It was a bet that I wouldn't have taken, knowing how powerful they were.

Some of the firm who hadn't gone to the party talked among themselves, saying that if it was true about Jack's murder, then surely this time the police would be asking questions. None of us had any idea then that they were not only asking questions, but also weaving a very deadly web.

It wasn't long before I got to hear the whole gruesome story of what led up to Jack's murder. I was told how the twins involved one of the Barry brothers, who owned the Regency Club. John, the elder brother, was always being called on by the firm for money and was rarely paid for any of the drink consumed in the club. He even had to open up a private bar for the firm to drink in. In this way, he could still keep his other customers coming to the club. Reggie had left a gun at the Regency and he had told John to put it away somewhere safe. On the night of the fateful party, he sent a message saying he wanted the gun brought to the party in Evering Road, which was only a short distance away from the club. Unfortunately for him, the younger brother was in charge that night, and when he received the message he knew he couldn't refuse to take it. Delivering that gun inadvertently got him involved, even though he didn't stay but went straight back to work. Jack was at the party by this time and, apparently, Reggie, spurred on by Ronnie, just opened fire on him. I heard that the trigger jammed on the gun.

When I met Hart, I let him know that Ian had told me what had taken place at the party. Hart said that Carol had worked hard trying to clean the place up, but the firm were arranging for it to be redecorated and carpeted – just to make sure that there was no trace of any blood left there.

It was only a couple of evenings later, while I was sitting talking to a friend in a club, that two men came in. They were strangers to me and I watched them go over to Billy and ask him if he knew where Reggie Kray was. They were big men and didn't look as though they were on a friendly mission. Billy was a little afraid to say too much to them so he came over to me and told me that the two men at the door were asking questions about Reggie, and would I mind asking them what they wanted him for.

I got up and walked over to them and asked if it was important that they see him.

'Yes, it is,' one of them replied, a little grim-faced. 'We want to know if it is true what we have heard, that he butchered Jack the Hat.'

The other man then interrupted and said unsmilingly, 'We did a bit of bird with him, and we don't think he was so bad that he deserved to be murdered.'

I had to be clever here – my answer could well make them decide whether or not to take their revenge on anybody connected with the firm. However, they prevented me from making any answer by repeating that they only wanted to see Reggie. I told them that I couldn't tell them where he was but thought the twins would be about in a few days. I offered to get a message to them and asked if there was any way the twins could get in touch with them.

One of them said: 'We will be around.'

I figured by the time they met up with Reggie they would have cooled off, but I went to see the twins where they were temporarily staying, out of the way, (I think probably I was the only person who knew they were in Walthamstow) and told Ronnie: 'Your uncle is getting worried. I have just come from the club. I just spoke to two geezers that came there looking for Reggie.'

'What do they want him for?' he asked.

'They didn't say, they just told me they were friends of Jack the Hat, and they seem to know that Reggie killed him. I am sure they are tooled-up.'

At these last words, Ronnie's face reddened and he shouted: 'That bastard had no friends. We have done everyone a favour getting rid of him. We were hearing from all sorts of people that he was gunning for us and we were told it was him or us. Those geezers must have been the law.'

He paused for a moment, then he laughed to himself. 'We have heard that they know there's been a murder, but they won't be able to do anyone for it – how can they prove anything without a body? He is well and truly burned up.'

It was kind of frightening, sitting there listening to him speaking so casually about somebody's death. He really thought they would get away with it once again.

Then he changed the subject. 'Where's Ian?' he asked.

'I don't know,' I replied. 'I haven't seen him for a few days. I will be going over to see him later – is there any message for him?'

'Yes,' he said, 'tell him to keep off the booze and be careful. We have a feeling that we are being watched, and tell him not to phone us: I think the phones are bugged.'

It was getting late, so I left Ronnie and drove over to see if Ian was in. He hadn't been around for a few days and I supposed he had been out drinking in some of his old haunts near to his flat. He was taking advantage of the twins' absence to see his old local pals with his girlfriend. I knocked on his door and waited for a few minutes before he answered. He looked surprised to see me there so late, but I followed him in and said: 'I have just come from Ronnie. He says you're to keep off the booze. He's scared in case you drop him in it over the Cornell shooting. They should be about again in a few days when the heat dies down.'

I reckoned that I had delivered enough messages for one day, so I said so long to Ian and went home, wondering what new events would take place the next day.

CHAPTER 14

OLD SCORES SETTLED

A few weeks passed, with the usual meetings going on in the pubs and clubs, and the twins came back on the scene again. It seemed as though Jack's murder had been forgotten.

Ronnie received a letter from a prisoner in a top-security prison (he didn't know him personally – Ronnie quite often was asked to help people), who had discovered that, while he was inside, his wife was having an affair with a man who worked in Romford Market, in Essex. He wanted to know if the firm could do something about it because he had still got a few years to serve and the thought of his home being broken up was driving him to depression. Ronnie promised the man that he would do what he could to help.

He called a meeting of a few members and said he

would like Connie to go and see this market man. However, Connie wasn't around – he never was when we wanted him. He had been with the firm for quite a few years and lately he seemed to have been clever enough to dodge getting more deeply involved. It looked as if he, too, was trying to pull out before it was too late.

In the end Ronnie decided to get Hart to go over to Romford and tell the man to stay away from the prisoner's wife, or he would find himself in a spot of bother.

'After all,' he said to Reggie, 'he did very well at the party when Jack the Hat got his lot.'

He turned to Hart and said: 'Come into the other room – I want to talk "privately".'

They were in there for about ten minutes, and when they emerged Hart didn't look his cheery self. He looked a bit red in the face, but nothing was explained to the rest of us.

All Ronnie said was: 'He is going over to Romford in a couple of days' time.'

Then he looked straight at me and said, 'You will drive him over there.'

As usual, there was no way that I could get out of it, but if anything had been planned, nothing was said to me.

The few remaining members of the firm seemed reluctant to speak their minds to one another. Experience had taught them to keep their thoughts to themselves, but I think we all knew that each day got us more involved and that we would all have to face the day of reckoning sooner or later. It was also getting difficult to keep in contact by phones because Ronnie insisted that the phones were bugged.

As I left the meeting, Ronnie came out to the door with me and said: 'Make sure that you are about when he has to go to see that geezer in Romford.'

'All right,' I replied, 'I will be at Dodger's club for the next few days. He can get me there.'

Sure enough, two days later, Hart came over to the club to see me. He said that he had just come from Ronnie, who had told him that the market man had his stall out and it would be the best time to see him.

'All right,' I said, 'I will take you over there now.'

We both left the club and, as I watched him get into my car, I noticed how nervous he was.

'What's the matter with you?' I asked. 'You look as if you'd seen a ghost. Are you ill?'

'No,' he said, 'I'm OK, but Ronnie told me to shoot that geezer.'

He stopped speaking and took out a Colt .45

revolver. I thought I must be seeing things, and my foot hit the brake.

'What the fuck are you doing with that gun?' My voice sounded slightly hysterical, so I tried to calm down. 'Don't you know we might be followed by the police?'

I started the car again and carried on driving towards Romford. Then I took a chance and said: 'Don't get involved by shooting this geezer. You won't get any help from anybody if someone yells for the police – and I don't want to be an accessory. The thing to do is to go back and tell them that this man has gone on holiday for a couple of weeks and has left his stall with someone else till he gets back. I will back you up.'

He was very hesitant about agreeing to this change of plan because he was scared to go against Ronnie's orders, and he didn't know if he could trust me, knowing that I was always with the twins.

'Will you really back me up?' he said, obviously turning things over in his mind. I nodded and he said, 'You had better drive me over there just to get a look at the place in case they have someone following me. At least then nobody can say that I never went there.'

I nodded in agreement, but told him it was only on condition that he either got rid of the gun or unloaded it. I stopped the car again and he tipped the bullets down a drain.

'I can't get rid of the gun,' he told me, 'it has come from Ronnie's arsenal. I will have to give it back.'

'Please yourself,' I said, 'but I shall stop at a café near the market and have a cup of tea while you go and look around. Meet me back there when you are through.'

He wasn't gone long and there was no shooting, but we did stick to our story that the man was on holiday and, luckily, that was the end of it.

Meanwhile, nobody had mentioned the murders for quite some time, and one evening when we were all in the pub Ronnie started talking very seriously about the various people who could go against him. Suddenly he said: 'I hear that Lennie has moved from the flat that we had Mitchell in.'

I was amazed at the way he seemed to get information about everybody connected to the firm. He had an uncanny way of knowing everything that went on.

'It wouldn't be a bad idea if he had an accident,' he continued, 'like falling from his fifth-floor flat.' His face lit up.

'I don't think you need to go that far,' I said. 'He would be too scared to go to the police.'

Ronnie looked at me and unfortunately I didn't see the danger signs, until I said: 'It's a pity you never paid him what you promised him. After all, he did hear the gunshots from outside his flat when Albert took Mitchell out to the van.'

'Don't fucking mention that mad bastard's name again,' he screamed at me. 'It is all forgotten – just like the others. No one will get done for them because no one will dare go to the police and give evidence against me.'

He stared round at all of us, then he simmered down again and decided to change the subject. 'We are going to have someone writing a book about us,' he said, laughing at his words. 'I don't think we can tell him everything when he comes into our company. We will just give him a free hand on all the good things that we do for the old people and for charities.'

Somebody asked: 'Where will he live while he is writing this book?'

'I have been told about a little flat round the corner to Vallance Road. He can stay there for a few weeks to give him the atmosphere of the East End. Tomorrow a few of us will go round and have a look at it and see if it is all right.'

The next day I drove him and a couple of others round to see this flat. As I approached it I remembered that my girlfriend and I had been here with Ian and his girl when they were flat-hunting, but they had not liked it. The flat was dark and dingy-looking and in a decaying block that should have been demolished years before.

As we walked in I said: 'Whoever is going to write this book must be mad to live in a hole like this.'

Ronnie laughed and said: 'He has agreed to stay here for a few weeks.' Then he added: 'We will have to get it cleaned up a bit first. Sammy and Harry Boy will be giving him some stories to write about.'

The following evening, there was a gathering of the firm at the Old Horns pub. We were all asked to be there and bring the women too because we were to be introduced to the man who was planning to write the book about the twins*. He was a quiet-spoken man and very polite. His name was John Pearson. We had been told to give him a free hand and to answer his questions – providing we did not discuss any of the violence that had taken place. The twins had arranged for him to speak to people who knew them in their young days, and I didn't see much of the author because I tended to take my girl to a local pub owned by a friend of mine. The parties

---

*Although only half-finished when the twins were arrested, the book was published in 1973 under the title of *The Profession of Violence*. I thought it was an interesting book.

with the firm went on and on and everybody seemed to drink too much.

I went round to see Ian one day to try to stop him from being out drinking every night. We inevitably started talking about Jack's murder again, and I said: 'I have heard that some of Jack's friends are out for revenge. If I were you, I would stay away from some of the meeting places.'

'Jack was a pal of mine too,' he said. 'If I had been at that party in Carol's place, I would have tried to stop it happening. Reggie wouldn't have killed him if Ronnie hadn't geed him up, and if he'd kept his mouth shut.'

'I agree with you,' I replied. 'Whenever there is a party arranged by Ronnie, it usually ends up with somebody getting done up. I bet their own cousin regrets coming out of the army and joining the firm – especially now they have got him involved in Jack's stabbing. Did you know that they even wanted him to shoot some geezer who was carrying on with someone's wife? I managed to talk him out of it.'

We both sat there talking about the past and we both knew that nobody would dare go into a witness stand and give evidence against the twins. But we also knew that unless something drastic happened, things would get a lot worse in the East End.

CHAPTER 15

'NO ONE CAN TOUCH US'

There was an air of discontent among the remaining members of the firm, who seemed to group together, resenting the few new faces that were now a part of our lives.

The protection money still came in, but not much of it seemed to be coming our way. Ronnie kept telling us that he was going to buy a big house in the country and when he spoke this way, I wondered whether he was pulling off deals without the rest of the firm knowing about it. I remembered the factory in Saffron Walden that made purple hearts. He could have made money there with Jeff, the friend who owned the big white Mercedes.

One evening we all decided to go to a basement

club in the West End, which was frequented by teams of villains from all over London. It was a club that the firm had an interest in (they put money into it and earned a percentage out of it) and sometimes we used it as a meeting place. When we walked in we noted how crowded it was but, as usual, we stood at the corner of the bar, drinking and smoking. All eyes turned to us and we were very watchful in case there was anybody out for revenge. It was hardly a night for relaxation.

After having a few drinks, Ronnie started egging the firm on to shoot Connie, towards whom he had a grievance; he seemed to suspect he was trying to draw away. Fortunately, Connie was in the Gents and nobody had any intention of taking up the offer. Ronnie had just started to call his name, when in walked brother Charlie. He listened to what was happening and whispered something to Ronnie, and then all three brothers left the club together. The rest of us stayed, prepared to spend the evening having a quiet drink and a chat.

The new members of the firm had been going round the pubs and clubs boasting to the owners that they were with the twins. At a nearby table, a man who was a stranger to us started shouting that he was now a member of the Kray firm. He had quite a crowd with him who were backing him up. Suddenly, without any warning, one of us drew a gun and shot the man in the leg. All hell let loose. It was like a free-for-all – the whole club got smashed up. When the fight was over everybody left, and what had started out as a nice quiet drink, ended as a fiasco.

The next morning the man who had done the shooting had to report to Ronnie, who liked to have all details of any aggravation that took place. Two weeks later, the club was closed down by the police. Yet each time one of the firm felt a police presence in a club, Ronnie would say: 'Nothing can touch us.'

I was still going to the gaming club where Ian and I had first met the twins' uncle when we had come down from Scotland and Billy also still frequented the club – but only when one of the firm's minders was there. That was the only time he felt safe. My girlfriend was pressurising me to dodge the firm's meetings, though, so I started to make excuses for my absences, mostly blaming my car for breaking down. Somebody warned me that a hand grenade was going to be thrown in one of our meeting places, but this never happened – although it did create a lot of tension within the firm. There were probably quite a few people in the East End who would have liked to send the firm to kingdom come, but they just didn't have the nerve. If they failed it would be their turn to face reprisals.

Ian came up to the club to see me one lunchtime with a message from Ronnie.

'He is having a party,' he told me, 'and he wants you there.'

I laughed. 'Who's going to get done tonight?'

It was a standing joke now with the firm whenever parties were mentioned.

'I'll be there,' I said. 'Where is it to be?'

'We will have a drink first in Blondy Bill's pub,' he answered.

I had no intention of going to this party in case it turned out to be another blood bath. After Ian left the club, I put the party out of my mind and settled down to a game of cards. I didn't go out that evening, but stayed in and watched television with my girl. At about 12.30 a.m. there was a knock on my door. I looked through the curtain and saw it was Hart. I watched for a few minutes before I opened the door, to make sure he was alone.

'What the fuck are you doing here?' I said furiously. 'And who gave you my address? No one but Ian has this address.'

He looked apologetic and replied: 'Ian is at the

party, he must have told them where you live. They have the needle with you for not showing up at the party. You and Connie are the only two missing. They sent me over to tell you that they want to see you.'

I shook my head and said: 'I'm not going out at this time of the night. Go back and tell them that you haven't seen me. You owe me a favour for backing you up when Ronnie wanted you to shoot that Romford geezer.' I paused for this to sink in, then I said: 'Look what happened to Jack when he was sent for to go to one of their parties. You know what they are like when they have had a good drink.'

He agreed with me and said: 'I will go back and tell them you are not in. But if I were you, I would move your car just in case they send someone else – now that they have this address. I am going back now – but for Christ's sake don't tell anybody that I saw you tonight.'

He said this last part nervously, so I replied: 'Don't worry, they will not hear it from me.'

After he left I went out and moved my car to a private car park, just in case I got another visitor. Sure enough, at about two o'clock in the morning, there was another knock at the door. This time I was in bed. I got up and checked the window to see who it was. Hart was standing there, so I dressed hurriedly and let him in again.

'They have sent me over again,' he said, looking fed up. 'They are both in the same kind of mood that they were in when Jack the Hat got done. I am marking your card because they are looking for blood and I don't want to get involved. They have even been trying to get somebody to bring Connie to the party.'

'It's not your fault,' I told him, annoyed that they were presumptuous enough to think I would want to get out of bed and go to a party. 'Ian shouldn't have given them my address.'

'I don't think he knew that they were going to send for you,' he said, and looked at his watch nervously.

It seemed to me that he had a lot of regrets about getting mixed up in Jack's stabbing and didn't want to get involved in any more. He had been going out with a nice girl and would have married her, but the twins liked to have her around at special parties to entertain their friends. She was a lively, pretty girl and thought the world of Hart.

When he left, he said that he would tell them I still wasn't home. Meanwhile, I prepared myself in case I got any more visitors during the night. I knew that once morning came and they sobered up, all thoughts of violence would be forgotten. It seemed as if drink brought out the worst in both of them – and unfortunately the worst always occurred in somebody else's house.

The next morning, I decided to go and see them, knowing that they would be in a normal frame of mind away from the booze of the night before. I knocked at their street door and it was Hart who opened it. He was surprised to see me standing there and looked at me in a quizzical way – but I just smiled and walked past him into the living room. I think he was wondering whether I was going to say something about seeing him the night before. He needn't have worried – I had no intention of dropping him in it.

Ronnie was scowling at me as I entered the room. 'Where were you last night? We wanted you to come to a big party.'

I had remembered that a few days earlier he had asked me to do a bit of nosing around to try to find out who it was that was making enquiries into the killing of Jack the Hat. So I said: 'You told me to go around and try to find out whether it was the law or local villains that were asking about Jack the Hat.'

He seemed to accept that and asked: 'Did you find out anything?'

'Yes,' I replied, 'everyone is saying that it was Reggie and Hart who killed him. There's a bit of talk going round that a little team are out to get them.'

'I have heard all that before,' said Reggie, who had been preparing to go out to see the Yank, who was in hospital. 'I will be back in an hour,' he called out.

Ronnie had now forgotten all about the party I had dodged the night before. We sat drinking and talking until Reggie came back from the hospital. Ronnie told me that the Yank had sent for Reggie to see him. He was in a private room, no nurses were about, and the way he kept on asking questions about the firm made the twins pretty certain that his conversation with Reggie that day was put on tape. When Reggie walked into the room after this visit, he went straight over to the trolley and poured himself a drink, which was unusual for him during the day. He looked a bit puzzled.

'I'm not sure if this is a trap – he didn't seem very ill and he was asking some funny kinds of questions.'

Ronnie sat thinking for a while, then he said: 'We will try to find out who he is working for and we will see to him.'

It wasn't often that he agreed with Reggie about anything, but I could see that this time he was getting concerned.

Meanwhile in a building called Tintagel House, in another part of London, a floor was set aside for the use of a special team of men, headed by Superintendents 'Nipper' Read and Harry Mooney. These were Regional Crime Squad top men, and this team had been working secretly around the clock to clear London of the Kray firm. Those hand-picked men worked efficiently and quietly, ready to pounce when the time was right. They knew that in order to get convictions, they had to get all the firm in custody at the same time. They also knew that if they were successful and were able to crack this most powerful team of villains, then London would be free of large pockets of organized crime and protection – and other people with similar ideas would be deterred.

Unknown to any of the firm, the Yank apparently was helping the team of police from Tintagel House, who knew about his various activities between the States and this country, including the sales of arms.

There was so much speculation among the members of the firm as to whether or not they were being watched and, if they were, by whom. Was it the law? Or people looking for a chance to seek revenge? I myself was only concerned at that time to make sure I wasn't at any parties held in anybody else's house.

Outsiders began to sense our vulnerability. There was some talk about up-and-coming young villains wanting to branch out and extract money from clubs that the firm had interests in. Ronnie reminded us to keep our ears open and to watch and see if any approaches were made to any of the club managers. If we saw anybody trying to muscle in we were to report it to him. However, if any other gangs did have ideas about taking over, they would soon have been put off because the firm were usually ready for any kind of aggro. There were still guns stashed in one of our regular haunts and one club had a gun hidden in the Ladies because the club had been raided by the police in the past and we knew that they wouldn't find it there.

The firm decided to test out whether or not they were being tailed by the police. The twins' mother had a caravan in Suffolk on the coast, and on many occasions she let members of the firm go for the day and use it. Going down to the caravan seemed a good way to find out once and for all. For a few weeks, everyone took it in turns to go and, sure enough, each car was followed. But it still didn't sink in that the firm weren't untouchable. They always thought that no matter what crimes they committed, they would always reign supreme, and although they thought the police were tailing them every so often, they never dreamt that they had a case almost prepared and witnesses ready to talk.

After a few weeks of this cat-and-mouse game, Ronnie sent for me and said: 'I've been checking up on who has been around lately and I haven't seen Bill. I want you to go round to his house and tell him that I want him to come to the pub tonight. I want to talk to him.'

'OK,' I said, and got into my car.

Bill lived in a small house just off Brick Lane, not far from the pub where we were meeting at that time. He was a man of modest means, with just a couple of suits, and he wasn't one to go round bragging about being with the firm. It was generally thought that the members of the firm all had fine wardrobes and flashy cars, but this wasn't so. We always looked well turned out, but we didn't always have much money in our pockets.

Bill looked very surprised when he answered the door and saw me standing there. I had hardly seen him since the Mitchell affair.

'Hello, Bill,' I greeted him. 'I've just come round to see how you are.'

His face brightened. 'Come in,' he said, 'would you like a cup of tea?'

'Yes, if it's no trouble,' I answered, following him into the kitchen. 'Ronnie wants to see you tonight at the pub. He hasn't seen you around lately.'

As I was speaking I noticed that he didn't look too well. He saw me watching him and said that he had been having a spot of trouble with his heart and couldn't always catch his breath.

'I am finished with them,' he told me suddenly. 'I have had enough. I've been loyal to them for years and now I have been ill and they didn't even send a few quid round for my wife. I don't care what happens, they will never use me again.' His outburst took me by surprise but he hadn't finished. 'I think they are through,' he said seriously. 'All they are getting round them now is a lot of idiots. You should try to get out before it's too late. Do you think they've forgotten about our involvement with Mitchell? Or that bird Lisa or Lennie? We all know too much. Either we will be reading about them in the papers or they will be reading about us.'

He stopped as suddenly as he started and I was amazed at the way he felt. He had never spoken so freely about the firm before and I started to get little warning signals. I thought back to when Reggie visited the Yank in hospital – he, too, had got warning signals. Were we all getting paranoid?

I decided to be on my guard and not talk too much – even though I had no real reason not to trust Bill. I got up to leave and said: 'Thanks for the tea. I will go back and tell Ronnie that you have been seeing a doctor and you can't go out yet.' I put my hand into my pocket and handed him a ten-pound note. 'Here, take this and have a drink,' I said.

Then I left the house and drove back to Ronnie. I told him that I had seen Bill and he didn't look well. Ronnie looked his usual serious self in the pub that night and although he accepted my story about Bill's illness, I could see he was not too pleased. He mentioned a few more names of people that hadn't been about recently, one of whom was the man called Charlie Clark, who had been given the gun to dispose of on the night Cornell got shot. He said he regretted giving him the gun because he had to take his word for it that the gun had been thrown into the river.

The firm was standing around in the bar just drinking, smoking and listening to Ronnie going through this list of men whom he had once trusted but now doubted. We all did our best to convince both him and ourselves that they wouldn't give evidence against the firm if approached by the police.

Life went on for us and the same routine prevailed,

collecting money from the clubs and having meetings to discuss if there were any new deals in the pipeline. If anybody noticed that the big-name celebrities no longer graced our company, they didn't say so. When Harry Boy or Sammy were asked to phone up one or two famous names they came back with a message that they were busy 'doing other things'.

Ronnie got bored with the lack of excitement and missed the film stars that we had so lavishly entertained in the past, so he decided that we should all have a night out at the Astor Club. This was a very nice nightspot in the West End and we were told to bring our wives or girlfriends along. Arrangements were made for us all to meet first in Blondy Bill's pub and to then go on to the Astor Club after closing time.

'I think we will show our few new firm members how to enjoy London's nightlife,' he said, feeling and looking more like a godfather with every word. I wondered at that moment whether the same words had been said for Ian and me about three years previously when we were the 'few new firm members'.

CHAPTER 16

THE DAWN SWOOP

My girlfriend was excited at the prospect of going to the nightclub. I had always tried to keep her out of the firm's company when it was 'party time' because I knew it really wasn't her kind of scene. But this was something different and we would just be like any other couple – out to have a good time.

I didn't have to drive Reggie or Ronnie that night – to my relief they had made other arrangements. We all met in the pub, as agreed. I didn't anticipate any trouble, but decided to drink little and keep my wits about me. There was quite a crowd of us and everybody was in a good mood. I looked around to see of any of the local police were about but I

223

couldn't see them. It went through my mind that it was strange that they weren't out drinking. Blondy Bill also noticed that there were none in the pub, and he commented on it to me. I hoped that no one was carrying a gun, especially since we all had women with us.

We left the pub at closing time and drove to the Astor Club in the West End. Everybody seemed to arrive at the same time but I had a habit of never parking my car outside any drinking place, so I stopped outside the club to let my girlfriend out. She went into the Astor with Reggie and his girl. After I had parked the car elsewhere, I walked to the entrance of the club. I had the oddest sensation of being watched, yet I didn't see anybody lurking around or even acting suspiciously. Maybe it was my Marine Commando training making me sensitive, but I had only felt like that once before, when I was in the Malayan jungle. There, too, I had been watched. I shrugged the feeling off and decided to have a good evening.

As I walked down the plush, carpeted staircase that led from the foyer to the main part of the club, where patrons could eat, dance and be entertained by a first-class cabaret, I saw not only the usual scantily dressed hostesses taking photos, but also a few strangers.

I took my seat beside my girl and she whispered to me: 'I think I had my photo taken with Reggie when I came in.'

'There do seem to be a lot of photos being taken,' I replied.

As I said that, Reggie shouted across to one of the girls with a camera: 'Stop taking photos. We don't want any tonight.'

He looked very annoyed. There were no more photos taken after that, but one or two of the firm suspected that some of these photographers were the law. Yet none of us noticed that we weren't offered any photos part-way through the evening. Normally, the practice was to develop the film right away and take them round the tables for the customers to buy photographs as mementoes.

We all ordered something to eat and sat back to enjoy the music and dancing. After the cabaret and a few more drinks, my girlfriend and I decided to leave. Ronnie was in deep conversation with a young man he had brought with him, and the others were all quite happily drinking and enjoying themselves. We called over to Reggie that we were going home – it was about two in the morning.

'Will you be round at the house in the morning?' he asked.

'No,' I said, laughing, 'leave it out. I will see you tomorrow night.'

My girl and I walked to the car and she commented that the evening had been one of the best nights she had spent in the firm's company. I agreed. It had been a good night. It was very late when we arrived back at our flat and we must have fallen asleep quickly.

It was noon when I woke up and my girl had gone out to do some shopping. There was a sudden banging on the door. I looked out of the window and saw Ian. I let him in – he was in a very excited state and was almost shouting.

'Have you heard what's happened? The twins have been nicked. There were about twenty cops – they broke into their mother's place when they were asleep. Ronnie was with a boy and Reggie was with his girl.'

He paused for his words to sink in. I was stunned. Although we had all felt from time to time that we were being followed, none of us really thought that the axe would fall so quickly. No wonder so many photographs had been taken in the Astor Club the night before – the police must have taken them straight back for developing.

'What will you do?' Ian asked. 'Will you leave London?'

'No, of course not,' I said, trying to look on the bright side. 'Why don't you wait and see what happens – they may not be kept in for very long – it might just be to answer a few questions. How about Charlie? Has he been picked up too?' I asked.

'Yes,' he replied, 'he was in bed, they must have timed it so that they were all in the same place at the same time.'

I thought back to all the little warnings that no one had heeded when we had felt that we were being watched or followed. Ronnie's words kept ringing in my ears. 'No one can touch us' he had said so many times.

'It's a good thing they don't know where we live,' he commented, 'or we would be nicked too.'

I agreed with that, but I knew that it would only be a matter of time before we, too, would be picked up.

'They can only charge me with harbouring Frank Mitchell,' I told him. 'I don't think that is worth hiding for the rest of my life for. I reckon they have already got to Bill. If they have, he will probably help them because he has the needle to the firm at the moment and he has already said that he wouldn't "take the can" for anybody. Not that I blame him – he is a sick man.' I paused for a moment to light a cigarette. 'Have you seen any of the rest of the firm yet?' I asked Ian, going through all the names.

'No,' he answered, 'I came straight round to see you.'

'What will you do if Ronnie gets charged with Cornell's murder?' I asked anxiously.

'I don't think he will be,' Ian replied. 'They may not get enough witnesses to come forward.' He sat thinking and then said: 'He once said that if he got done he would plead guilty and get me out of it.'

I laughed at this. 'No one pleads guilty to murder.'

'What are you going to do?' he asked.

'Nothing,' I replied. 'I am not running away – there is nowhere to go. I will stay here and see what happens. If they haven't been charged after forty-eight hours they will have to let them go. I wish I knew if anybody else has been nicked. If Ronnie does get done for murder, you should give yourself up.'

'What for?' Ian asked. 'They have nothing on me.'

I looked doubtfully at him, then I said: 'I reckon the police have been on our tail for months. I think we had better have a drink, it might be our last for a long time.'

I poured out a couple of scotches and we sat there just thinking our own thoughts and chewing over the events of the past few years since we came to London and joined up with the firm. In a way I was slightly relieved it was coming to an end, because if I did get arrested and had to serve a sentence, at least after that I could settle down and start life afresh.

'I once asked Albert if he shot Mitchell,' I said, 'but he told me he didn't.'

Ian looked up. 'When did you ask him that?'

'Oh, the night you and he had a fight at the Regency Club when you were both drunk. I had to get between you – I bet you didn't even know he had a gun on him that night.'

'No,' he said, 'I didn't.'

As we finished speaking there was a tap on the window and we both jumped. I got up to see who it was, but it was only my girl with Hart's girl, whom she had met while out shopping. They couldn't get in the door quick enough to tell us what we already knew. I asked if Hart had been arrested but she said not as far as she knew. She only stayed a moment, then hurried home.

I went to the phone and called the twins' flat – no answer. I dialled the club and asked if any of the firm were there, but got no joy. I decided to leave it for the moment and phone the pub later, but as Ian left, I told him to be careful and not go to the pub for a few nights until we were sure of the facts about the twins' arrests.

The next morning I decided to visit the gaming club in Brick Lane where it had all begun for Ian and myself three years previously. I walked up the familiar narrow staircase wondering how long it would be before my visits here would end. I could smell food from the little café next door, and wondered why I had not noticed it before. I suppose I had been too busy thinking about cards and going on meets to give anything else a second thought.

Billy, the twins' uncle, greeted me at the door with a shocked look on his face. 'What are you doing here? Don't you know that the twins have been arrested? The Old Bill have been here – they are looking for you. If I were you, I would stay out of the way till they sort things out. I reckon the twins will be out soon on bail.'

He sounded optimistic, but I wasn't so sure. I had a very strong feeling that the police had done their homework well and that soon I and the rest of the firm would be standing together in the dock.

I told him that he should stay at home for a while just in case of reprisals by people who could take advantage of the twins' absence by getting their own back on him. He smiled, but I knew I was right.

'Do you need any money?' he asked. 'I can let you have a few quid.'

I shook my head and said, 'Thanks, but I don't need any.'

Dodger, the owner of the club, came over and also offered me some money, but I refused and said, 'What's the good of it? I have a feeling it won't be long before I am picked up.'

As I was leaving, I called out to a few of the men playing cards, 'I'll be seeing you,' but I wasn't very hopeful.

The next few days were spent with my girl, and going to my pal Blondy Bill's pub and chatting to him and his wife. I didn't try to hide. One afternoon, my girl reminded me that we were to go to a family party at her sister's house. I told her that it would be best if she went alone. Her family didn't know about my past and I didn't want them involved in my immediate future. I popped into the pub before dropping her off at her sister's house and I noticed the local cop having his usual quiet pint. Bill asked if many of the firm had been arrested.

'I don't know,' I told him. 'I will be back later – I am just going somewhere.'

When I got back to the flat to pick her up she was looking upset. 'I don't like to leave you,' she said. 'Please stay in while I am gone.'

'I will just have a drink in Bill's pub,' I told her. I

didn't mention that I had seen the local cop there in the afternoon. 'The police can't know where I live,' I said, 'or they would have been here by now.'

She brightened up and we got into the car. As she was getting out of the vehicle at her sister's house, I said: 'Phone me when you want to leave.'

But she said: 'Don't worry, I will get a lift back.'

I drove back to Stoke Newington and parked my car round the back of the pub, where I always parked. I looked round and saw two other parked cars; both had men sitting in them. Somehow I knew it was the law, but I felt that if I were going to be picked up, I would rather it was when I was alone and not at home with my girl.

The local cop was still sitting in the same place when I walked in. 'Hello, I see you're still here.'

He looked up and nodded.

I looked around the bar and saw the two strangers at the far end. I called out to Bill: 'I'll have a double scotch.'

He looked nervous, and said: 'Have this on the house.'

The local cop got up and went outside. I suppose he went to tell the others that I was in. As I was having my drink, one of the strangers went to the Gents and as he passed me I could hear his walkie-talkie crackling in his pocket. He was only gone about thirty seconds when the pub doors opened and in burst about ten plain-clothes cops. They took positions around the pub and every one must have been hand-picked – they were all six-footers and looked ready for anything. One man came forward and walked over to where I was having my drink. He was tall, clean cut and very smartly dressed, as were the men with him.

'Hello,' he said, very politely, 'my name is Superintendent Mooney.'

I realized then that this must be the big Irishman that we had heard about months ago, through the grapevine, making enquiries about the Kray firm. I couldn't believe at first that he was a high-ranking policeman – he looked more like a bank manager and was very quietly spoken.

I put up my hands to indicate that I wasn't carrying a gun and I didn't speak as two of his men searched me. Then he said: 'You will have to come along with me.'

'Of course,' I answered.

He beckoned to a couple of his men to take me outside. I expected them to handcuff me, but they didn't. When we got outside I knew why. There were about twenty police in the street, all quietly waiting.

The passers-by must have thought a film was being made, or that a crime had been committed on a large scale. I didn't try to run for it – if I had I would probably have been shot and I presumed they were all armed.

One of them said: 'Where is your car?'

'You must know where it is,' I replied, 'you saw me arrive.'

I pointed to the back of the pub, where my car was parked. When we got round there I saw that the two cars parked there when I arrived were now hemming my car in.

'Where are your keys?' asked Superintendent Mooney. 'We will take care of your car.'

I gave him my keys and told him where I lived. I was told to get in a car, and two of the police sat in the front with one on either side of me in the back. One of them must have wanted to make a name for himself because he told me that if I made a move he would shoot me and then they would say I had been trying to escape. I just looked at him, knowing that he was trying to be big.

'I don't think you will do anything like that – you would have to answer to your chief.'

One of the men in the front turned round and

told him to shut up, which he did, but I never saw him again.

I was taken to Stoke Newington police station and put into an office. I was allowed to smoke and after about twenty minutes Superintendent Mooney came in and asked me if I would like some tea, which he must have ordered already because at that moment a policewoman came in with it.

'We have been looking for you for days,' he said.

'I haven't been hiding,' I told him. 'I have been to the club and the pub where you picked me up tonight.'

After a few preliminary questions, I was taken to a police station in the West End, where I was questioned about Frank Mitchell. Everybody was friendly and polite, and having heard so many stories about police brutality, I wondered if perhaps they had orders to be gentle with the firm. I was put in a cell for the night and early in the morning I had my first encounter with Superintendent Mooney's partner, Read. The cell was unlocked and in walked two men. The shorter of the two said to me: 'My name is Superintendent Read, and this is Chief Inspector Cater.'

I looked at him and thought, so this is the famous 'Nipper' Read. I had heard so much about him from

Ronnie in the last three years, that I felt I knew him personally. He had been trying to nail the firm for some time – since long before Ian and I came on the scene. Ronnie once had a pet snake and he called it Nipper Read from the Yard. He didn't look like the stereotype policeman. He was short and pleasant-looking. He was also, like Superintendent Mooney, very quiet-spoken and polite.

'You will be going to court this morning, and you will be charged with harbouring Frank Mitchell,' he told me.

I didn't say anything – I didn't have to.

After breakfast they took me to a different cell. Two minutes later the door was opened and in walked the twins and Charlie. They looked as surprised as I felt when they saw me sitting on the bed smoking. I stood up, and was just going to speak, when Ronnie put his finger to his mouth to silence me. The door was closed, leaving the four of us alone. Ronnie then started to check over the cell to see if it was bugged. He looked at the bars on the window, the light bulb and even under the bed. While he was doing this, we stood silently watching. Only when he satisfied himself that it was OK did he relax and start to speak.

'How long have you been here?' he asked. 'What have they got you for?'

At that time none of us had any idea that most of the firm were now in custody.

'I am going to be charged with harbouring Mitchell,' I told them grimly.

Ronnie looked surprised. 'How can you be?' he asked. 'Who has grassed? No one will dare give evidence against us.'

He really seemed to believe his own words. He and Reggie went through the names of the people who could connect them to Frank Mitchell's disappearance. They acted as though he really had gone into hiding and would suddenly reappear. We went over the names, not knowing that the police had already got statements from most of the people connected with the Mitchell episode.

'What about Lennie?' I asked.

The look on Charlie's face told me that Lennie could point the finger at him. He sat on the bed, deep in thought. None of us spoke for a few minutes, then Ronnie said: 'Do you know if Bill's been pulled in?'

'I don't know,' I replied, 'I went to his house a few days ago but no one was in.'

Ronnie looked more confident and said: 'He is probably keeping out of the way.'

Reggie came over to me and whispered: 'Have they asked you anything about Jack the Hat?'

'Yes,' I replied, 'his name was mentioned by "Nipper" Read just before I was brought down here.'

He looked worried. 'Have they got Hart?' he asked.

'I don't know who they've got,' I answered.

He started to ask something else, but was interrupted by the cell door being unlocked. We were led upstairs and I have never before seen so many policemen in one place as I saw on that short walk. They were all big and in uniform – and they lined the stairway. Then I saw coming out of the other cells various men who had been arrested. Ian was not with them.

We all stood in the dock together at Bow Street, and then the police brought in a witness. It was Bill. There was a shocked gasp from Ronnie and Reggie – they just couldn't believe it. He gave evidence saying he was one of the men who harboured Frank Mitchell for the Kray twins. I thought that he looked ill – he must have had guts to stand there, knowing what power the twins had, he could be dead before he ever went to court again.

As we went down to the cells, Ronnie said: 'That dirty bastard. He won't get away with it.'

We were all remanded for seven days and were separated. After going backward and forward from our various prisons to Bow Street, with full escort and sirens blaring, we were committed to trial at the Old Bailey. Ronnie was charged with the murder of George Cornell; Reggie was charged with the murder of Jack McVitie.

I had plenty of time to think about the predicament that I was in. By now I knew that there was 'no honour among thieves'. It was July 1968 – four years since Ian and I had come to London to start a new life.

Ian had now been arrested and charged with being an accessory to murder. He and his girl had moved to another part of London and didn't get picked up until over a week later, when he went into the East End to drink in one of the places known to the police. We had been kept apart from the twins in the early stages of the trial and one day, while exercising, I managed to talk to him. He said he had heard that the police didn't have enough evidence to convict Ronnie of Cornell's murder and that they would probably both get off.

I looked at him in disbelief and said: 'You are a fool. You should tell "Nipper" Read the truth – you didn't fire that gun.'

My words fell on deaf ears. He stubbornly insisted that Ronnie would plead guilty which would mean a lesser sentence for Ian, given the fact he did not fire the shot that killed Cornell.

'How did you get picked up, anyway?' I asked. 'I thought you had moved and would stay out of the way until it was all over.'

He looked sheepish. 'I got drunk one night and I saw Charlie Clark. I think he must have told the police what pub I was in because they came for me.'

Ian was eventually sentenced to twenty years, which as far as I know, he spent in Durham Prison. Our paths haven't crossed since.

At about 11 o'clock one evening, I was taken by the warder to an office. When I entered, I saw it was occupied by Superintendent Mooney and a detective. He told me to sit down and I felt quite relaxed. We started talking and he said nothing was going to be written down; it was strictly off the cuff. He told me that Lisa, Lennie and Bill were Crown witnesses.

'Do you really think that you can keep them safe during the trial?' I asked.

He assured me that a lot of money was being spent on protecting the witnesses in case there was anybody around with orders to silence them. It sounded as though they had been protecting some of their witnesses for some time before the firm's arrest. He also told me that Hart and Albert had already given statements. Hart gave a statement about the gruesome murder of Jack the Hat. He saved himself from going to prison by turning Queen's evidence. He really had very little choice. Albert gave evidence about the twins' organizing Frank Mitchell's escape. He was sentenced to three years for his involvement. There was not enough evidence to pin Mitchell's murder on anybody and I was never asked to give evidence on the Mitchell affair. I realized then that the net had closed.

'I shall plead guilty to harbouring Mitchell, but what are my chances for getting bail? After all, I have a girl on the outside and I have to think of her safety.'

Mooney nodded and said: 'We will give her the same protection as the other women.'

I thanked him and went back to my cell. I applied for bail at the next hearing and got it, even though I knew that I would have to serve a short sentence for my part in the Frank Mitchell episode.

The trial that had started at the Old Bailey on 5 March 1969 took place in the Number One Court Room and was presided over by Judge Melford Stevenson. The Court was packed every day – not only downstairs, where the solicitors, barristers and defendants sat, but upstairs in the public gallery, which was lined with the families and many friends of the firm. At the back of the court were the newspaper reporters. The jury sat enthralled.

The trial lasted nine months, and was one of the most expensive and sensational ever. The witnesses and their families and members of the jury were all offered police protection twenty-four hours a day. The police gave them all new addresses (though not new names) and plain-clothes detectives – some male, some female – accompanied the witnesses and their families everywhere they went, right round the clock. All this was paid for by the Regional Crime Squad.

The witnesses never appeared in the stand together. They were brought in one by one by detectives. Out of court too they were kept in separate rooms and away from the photographers and journalists. After they had given their evidence for the prosecution, they were taken away from the Old Bailey. None of them was recalled, but they were protected till the end of the trial.

The witnesses for the Crown, as Superintendent Mooney had told me, included Bill, Lisa and Lennie. They testified that I was in the flat with them when Frank Mitchell was taken out and they heard the shots. I had no option but to plead guilty. None of them received a sentence.

The defendants were quiet during the trial, except once when Ronnie (at least, this is what I've heard) lost his cool and went into the witness box where he called one of the barristers a fat slob. Otherwise he remained impassive as always.

In the end the roll call of sentences for the Krays went like this: Ronnie received a recommended thirty-year sentence which he is serving in Broadmoor; Reggie received a recommended thirty-year sentence which he is currently serving in Parkhurst; Charlie received a ten-year sentence for disposing of Jack's body (he is now out of prison and is a businessman). There were no appeals.

By the time I got bail my girl had moved to a different flat, and here I was taken. She had been staying there with a plain-clothes policewoman. I got quite a shock when I got there because it turned out to be in the same block in Finchley as the one Ronnie had stayed in when he planned Mitchell's escape.

After the trial was all over and I had paid my dues to society, I met the club owner who had stood bail for me.

'I am glad that it happened,' he said, referring to the arrests and the trial. 'I am going to make sure that I never pay protection money to anybody again. The police worked hard to make the East End safe for people like me by putting the twins away.'

'Yes,' I replied, 'you are right. If some of the firm hadn't gone down for murder things would have got worse. It's only a pity that Ian went down with Ronnie over Cornell's shooting. He didn't do it.'

'Supposing Reggie had pleaded guilty to Jack's murder?' he said.

'Then Hart would have gone down with him,' I answered. 'He boasted about what happened at that party enough times when he thought they had got away with it. He really wanted to be a big-time gangster like his uncles.'

Rumours continued to circulate in London about the disappearance of the bodies of Mitchell and Jack the Hat. Some said they were taken to a pig farm; others said they had been put in cement and were holding up the Bow flyover in the East End. But my theory was that they were cremated in a proper cemetery. Those questions were never answered.

We started thinking about Albert, and my club-owner friend said: 'Did you know that Albert used to work for me in the club before he joined up with the firm?'

'Yes – I did know,' I replied. 'I think he only came

on the firm to wait for revenge after he got shot in the foot by Reggie some time ago.'

I paused, and he broke in with: 'That trial was really sensational. It must have been the most expensive and successful case in history. The protection of witnesses and their families was so well thought out.'

I nodded, but my mind was still on Mitchell's disappearance, and I said: 'I wonder who really shot the Mad Axeman. I know Albert gave a statement to the police, and he didn't do it. No one really knows the truth, except the people in the van at the time. It is a mystery that will probably go down in the files as the murder without conviction.'